REVOLUTION

Volume 6

THE CHALLENGE ROAD

THE CHALLENGE ROAD

Women and the Eritrean Revolution

AMRIT WILSON

LONDON AND NEW YORK

First published in 1991 by Earthscan Ltd.

This edition first published in 2022
by Routledge
4 Park Square, Milton Park, Abingdon, Oxon OX14 4RN

and by Routledge
605 Third Avenue, New York, NY 10158

Routledge is an imprint of the Taylor & Francis Group, an informa business

© 1991 Amrit Wilson

All rights reserved. No part of this book may be reprinted or reproduced or utilised in any form or by any electronic, mechanical, or other means, now known or hereafter invented, including photocopying and recording, or in any information storage or retrieval system, without permission in writing from the publishers.

Trademark notice: Product or corporate names may be trademarks or registered trademarks, and are used only for identification and explanation without intent to infringe.

British Library Cataloguing in Publication Data
A catalogue record for this book is available from the British Library

ISBN: 978-1-032-12623-4 (Set)
ISBN: 978-1-003-26095-0 (Set) (ebk)
ISBN: 978-1-032-19042-6 (Volume 6) (hbk)
ISBN: 978-1-032-19043-3 (Volume 6) (pbk)
ISBN: 978-1-003-25747-9 (Volume 6) (ebk)

DOI: 10.4324/9781003257479

Publisher's Note
The publisher has gone to great lengths to ensure the quality of this reprint but points out that some imperfections in the original copies may be apparent.

Disclaimer
The publisher has made every effort to trace copyright holders and would welcome correspondence from those they have been unable to trace.

THE CHALLENGE ROAD

Women and the Eritrean Revolution

Amrit Wilson

First Printing, 1991

Copyright (c) Amrit Wilson, 1991

All rights reserved. No part of this publication may be reproduced, stored in a retrieval system or transmitted in any form or by any means electronic, mechanical, photocopying, recording or otherwise without the prior written permission of the publisher.

Originated by Earthscan Ltd.

Cover Design by Carles Juzang

Library of Congress Catalog Card Number: 91-60850

ISBN: 0-932415-71-7 Cloth
0-932415-72-5 Paper

For the fighting women of Eritrea – no matter where and how they fight their battles

Contents

1. Introduction — 1
2. Mabrat's Story — 9
3. Laying the Foundations — 33
4. Behind the Enemy Lines — 62
5. Fighters — 87
6. Land Reform — 111
7. Marriage — 122
8. Health — 139
9. The Future — 150
   Appendices — 155
   References and Notes — 198
   Index — 205

Acknowledgements

I would like to thank the many Eritrean women whose experiences, perceptions and analysis have inspired and created this book; the National Union of Eritrean Women for giving me their precious time, guiding me and looking after me in the liberated zone; Askalu Menkarios, without whose encouragement I would never have embarked on this book, and Worku Zerai, who took me round the liberated zone, showed me Eritrea through her eyes and gave me the confidence to complete this project.

I am also grateful to the EPLF office and the NUEW in London for their support and for checking parts of the manuscript; to Abdulrahman Mohamed Babu for his insights into revolutionary strategy; and to Trish Silkin for allowing me access to her research.

Finally I would like to thank my daughter, Kalpana, for many stimulating discussions which helped me understand the lessons of the Eritrean struggle for us in South Asia.

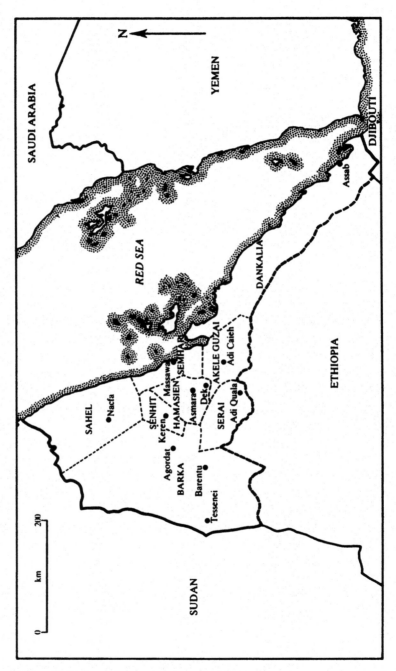

Map 1: Eritrea's provinces and towns

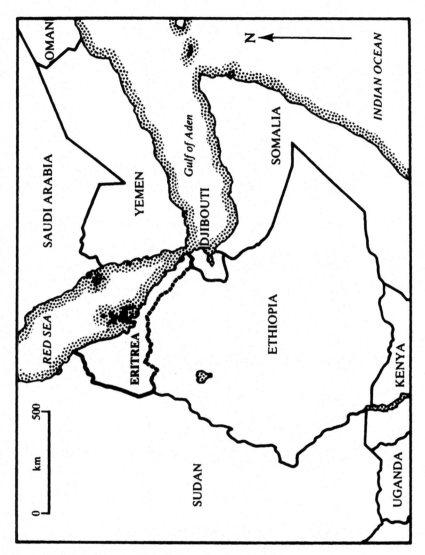

Map 2: Eritrea: in the Horn of Africa

Abbreviations and Acronyms

ELF	Eritrean Liberation Front
ELM	Eritrean Liberation Movement (Group of Seven)
EPHP	Eritrean Public Health Programme
EPLA	Eritrean People's Liberation Army
EPLF	Eritrean People's Liberation Front
EPRP	Ethiopian People's Revolutionary Party
NUEW	National Union of Eritrean Women
PLC	Party of Love of Country
SDF	Sudan Defence Force
SUEE	Society for the Unification of Eritrea and Ethiopia
TPLF	Tigrayan People's Liberation Front
UN	United Nations

1 Introduction

> Remember the women who have been martyred fighting. Remember the women who gave birth while feeling from their homes, and those women who have been born and have grown up fighting for the liberation of our country. We *are* the EPLF as much as anyone . . . We fight for our rights as women, but the world outside our bodies, outside our identity as women, belongs to us too.

It was one of those unforgettable conversations so common in Eritrea through which people try in different ways to explain the meaning of the revolution. Maaza, a cadre from the women's mass organization, expressed it this way. Others speak of particular battles in the anti-colonial struggle, or of changes in power structures, or of the love and support of their comrades. Each story elaborates and extends the same theme about how the people of Eritrea experience, create and pilot their struggle – how they made the Eritrean revolution and what the Eritrean revolution made them.

Eritrea lies like a long, wide dagger above the northern flank of Ethiopia, stretching from the entrance to the Red Sea to a point nearly half way along it. It is remarkable in many ways. What other country has confronted a colonizer backed first by the United States then the Soviet Union? Where can one see such immense diversity of culture united in such a powerful revolutionary nationalism? What other revolution in recent times has had such extensive liberated areas, and where, above all else, has the struggle for liberation been so long and so intense?

2   The Challenge Road: Women and the Eritrean Revolution

In Eritrea the struggle determines and illuminates everything. Every view of the land is drawn powerfully into focus by it: the green plateau and rich dark soil of the highlands where the densely populated villages have been bombed and burnt mercilessly by the Ethiopian forces; and the vast desert lowlands, the ideal guerrilla base, which hold within them all the pain, sacrifice and momentum of the struggle. Here in the lowlands the drone of an Ethiopian Antonov on a surveillance and bombing mission can still be heard every nightfall and dawn. Every encounter on the long road brings a new picture of a people's resistance: nomads kneeling in prayer with Kalashnikovs strapped to their backs; a huge Soviet truck converted into a water-carrier sheltering under the foliage of trees until it is safe to move at night; or members of the people's militia appearing suddenly out of the dark.

Twenty-nine years of struggle have had a major impact on the identity of the people. They have not only engendered an intense nationalism but have subtly and crucially altered it, giving it a revolutionary form. Perhaps as a result, particularly in the areas where the Eritrean People's Liberation Front (EPLF) has had a long presence, we no longer see the sharp cutting dichotomy between the personal struggle of women and the broader politics of national struggle so common elsewhere in the world. Here, intense personal identities are drawn into a no-less intense collective identity, so no one speaks purely for her- or himself any more.

Yet in Eritrea there is no uniformity, and nor can there be any. Even among the women fighters of the EPLF there is a wide variety of backgrounds and communities. Their families may be city dwellers, traders, nomadic pastoralists or communal farmers. They may belong to anyone of Eritrea's nine major ethnic "nationalities" – Tigrinya, Tigre, Beja, Kunama, Nara, Billen, Saho, Afar or Rashaida – each with its characteristic traditional culture and language. Together as Eritreans these different groups have in the last hundred years or so experienced a series of colonial oppressors – the Italians, the British and the Ethiopians.

But what was their experience in the period before Italian colonialism? The Ethiopians have claimed that they ruled Eritrea before the Italians, but this is a blatant fabrication, a typical colonial version of history.

In the third century AD the area of present-day Eritrea was the seat of the Aksumite Kingdom, a major commercial and trading power centred round a port of legendary fame at Adulis. When the Aksumite Kingdom declined the region became divided into a variety of kingdoms, until in the fourteenth century a major part of it was united again as the Medri-Bahri or "land of the sea". It was divided from Ethiopia, or Abyssinia as it was then called, by the River Mareb, and ruled by an elected leader the Bahri Negassi. Local wars continued, however, and in the sixteenth century as the Ottoman Empire expanded into the area it was able to take Massawa, a major port on the Red Sea. Eritrea was now divided between the Turks and dynasties from Sudan.

With the opening of the Suez Canal in 1869, the Egyptians joined the other military powers jockeying for control of the Horn of Africa. They occupied Massawa, Karen and south-central Eritrea and began to move into areas held by the Turks. They also tried to invade Abyssinia but were disastrously defeated in battles at Gura and Gundut, Eritrean towns near the Ethiopian border. Following this, parts of the Eritrean highlands were controlled by Ethiopia for 13 years until in 1889 Emperor Yohannes of Abyssinia was killed in a battle with Sudanese forces. By now Italy had gained a foothold in the region. It had managed to take Massawa from the Egyptians and was pushing into the interior of the region (which it called Eritrea or Red, after the sea), despite protests from the Turks and Egyptians. As Margery Perham wrote,[1] it is clear that "it was not from Ethiopia but from the collapsing Egyptian empire that the Italians took Massawa and that the Egyptians had themselves taken it over from the Turks".

Beneath the successive waves of invasions by foreign forces which ranged from Ethiopian feudalism to European capitalism, Eritrea remained a land of many nationalities. These groups were fragmented into smaller entities ruled by various types of overlords – *ra-ises*, *deglals*, *bahri-negasis* and *sultans*. Their socio-economic development, as an EPLF document states, "to some degree varied from nationality to nationality and ranged from the lowest form of semi-primitive communal herding to the highest form of semi-feudal farming".[2]

With the arrival of the Italians, colonial capitalism began to interact directly and indirectly with the modes of production of all these groups, giving rise to new contradictions which created new classes and released new social forces. These classes and social forces launched the struggle against colonialism which was to consolidate the modern Eritrean nation.

The contradictions created by colonialism will be discussed in detail later in this book; at this point I would like to emphasise only that they affected the whole country, although in very different ways in different areas. In the highlands, towns were established by the colonialists and capital was invested, as a result of which a working class emerged, largely from the peasantry of the surrounding areas. In the lowlands where large areas of land were appropriated by the Italians, mainly for plantations, and where conflicts between existing tribal entities were intense in the pre-colonial period, the impact of colonialism and the process of formation of new classes were more complex. For example, in the Western lowlands military protection was the obligation of dominant clans within a tribe of goat-and camel-herders. Here the *pax Italiana* imposed by colonialism, together with better veterinary services, led to a weakening in the relations of dominance and the formation of a new class of people freed from their former servitude.[3]

Another example is from Barka where two quite different nationalities, the animist Naras and the Muslim Tigre-speaking Beni-Amer, had lived in conflict for years. The *pax Italiana* led to a very different interaction there. Trade between the two groups began to flourish, and eventually the Naras converted to Islam and changed from a system of communal farming to a less egalitarian form where the elected leader was replaced by a hereditary official who now represented the interests of the Italians.[4]

The impact of colonialism on women's lives was enormous. The women who migrated to the towns ended up in highly exploitative and often degrading employment, working for example as domestic servants, bar-women or low-paid factory workers. Even in areas with no migration there were major changes.[4] In Barka, for example, Nara women who played (and still play) a vital and recognized economic role continued to be consulted over family decisions, but now they were expected to be veiled and quiet in the presence of men. In general, in every region and every nationality women's oppression within the family was intensified by colonialism – because here, in contrast to the metropolitan countries, capitalism retained and sometimes extended feudal and semi-feudal relationships, modifying them as needed and incorporating them within its own exploitative framework.

Family structure continued to be more or less the same as before (although tensions between families increased), and with the exception of the more communally orientated and animist groups, families remained intensely patriarchal.

As in all patriarchal peasant societies, the woman's main role was to produce sons: – in her womb lay the crucially important but uncontrollable and therefore mysterious ability to strengthen and propagate the patriarchal line. Her role was therefore perceived by society as being wholly tied to her "natural activities": the production and rearing of children. Since these were not seen as work she was not regarded as a worker, despite her labour on her husband's fields and pastures. This labour was hard and unremitting. Survival in a peasant society is always hard but in Eritrea's agricultural and pastoral communities it is particularly so, because of the uncertainty of the weather and the shortage of land. As a male EPLF cadre who had once been a middle peasant told me: "a man who does not wake up early is ostracized". For the woman the day is longer still. A woman from the highlands, now a fighter, told me about her mother's day:

> My mother would get up early before anyone else. She would do all the housework, the cleaning and the cooking which takes hours, and the fetching of water from a long distance. And then she would

work in the fields doing jobs which are not considered heavy but are very tiring like weeding, cleaning, cutting and so on. When my father came back from the fields she would wash his feet in a bowl of warm water. She would be the last to go to bed. . . . There is a proverb which says that asking a woman to rest is like making a donkey your guest.

It is the same in the semi-nomadic communities in the lowlands. Here the hardest time of year is when the family leave their highland home and start their summer journey to the lowlands. As Fatma Omer from Rora Bagla told me:

> The woman dismantles the tent which is in front of the house and loads it on to an ox or donkey. Then she gets the children ready and attends to the goats. The kitchen utensils are also packed on the donkey. Whenever they stop she has to set up the tent, prepare the food and look after the animals and children. The man comes and sleeps. She has to make porridge and coffee, then she feeds him. He eats alone or sometimes with the children. If he leaves anything she eats it. During the night they move again. It is the same process all over again. It takes ten days to reach the lowlands north or north-east of Hashkerbeb.

Here girls are sometimes engaged when they are still in their mother's wombs and often before they reach puberty. As in other patriarchal peasant societies, pregnant women are looked after with care and affection but the sex of the child they produce is crucial. As a woman from the out skirts of Asmara told me:

> The mother of a son is congratulated and given presents. There is ullulation and feasting. If a girl is born there is ullulation too but only three times, not seven as in the case of a boy. The neighbours who help with the birth do not congratulate the mother of a girl, instead they console her and she gets depressed. If a woman has only girls she is regarded as a failure. Then the man can justify marrying again – it is allowed among orthodox Christians and Muslims, otherwise they can secretly have another wife.

If the birth of a girl is seen in a negative light, her childhood reinforces it. She is prepared by her family and by her religion, Christian or Muslim, for her life as a married woman.

She is secluded to varying extents depending on her religion, and she is circumcised in an attempt to control her sexuality and sexual activities. She is taught to be withdrawn, obedient and passive, and to believe that she is inferior to men. At the same time she learns that she is the guardian of family honour which is highly sensitive to her behaviour and her chastity.

However, it is always difficult to generalize, in Eritrea partly because there is such a wide variety of cultures and partly because within each group there are always many exceptions. The above description broadly defines what tradition demands from women in patriarchal families, the norm for the majority of Muslim and Christian communities in Eritrea. The exceptions are the Kunama and to a lesser extent the Nara communal societies with their collective agriculture and women-centred families. Each kind of family structure originates from a particular stage of development and is further shaped by external influences and internal interactions. Within each group there are also the variations caused by class and by affluence or poverty. In Eritrea there are no acute inequalities – no big landlords on the scale of Asia or Latin America – but as in most other societies where feudal attitudes persist, affluence and family prestige make the woman even more of a possession of her husband's family.

I have briefly described some of the varied contradictions engendered by the years of Italian colonialism. This phase was to end after Italy's defeat early in the Second World War. Eritrea was then taken over by the British who ruthlessly exploited it for 11 years (see Chapter 2). By the time they finally left in 1952 they had dealt the country a serious economic blow by dismantling and selling off around $86 million worth of industrial equipment, some of which had been set up during the war. Eritrea was federated to Ethiopia by the United Nations in the face of massive protests and against all historical and legal considerations – the reason was that the West and particularly the United States wanted to retain control of the region through its client regime in Ethiopia.

Under Emperor Haile Selassie Ethiopia was an autocratic state, but it was also a neocolony of the type more commonly found in southern Asia than in Africa. It was a country where on the one hand foreign capital had been invited in and had ruthlessly exploited the people and on the other hand feudal values had been retained and re-created, sometimes reshaped in line with the needs of rulers, both indigenous and foreign. The result was a peculiarly violent power structure with all the arrogance, revenge and cruelty of feudalism but with none of its obligations. As we shall see in later chapters, as a colonizer such a country is an entirely and ruthlessly destructive force.

For Eritrea, federation with Ethiopia brought no federal rights but an army of occupation, followed after 11 years of savage repression by formal colonization through annexation. The change in the Ethiopian regime – the overthrow of Haile Selassie, the emergence of the Dergue (the ruling military junta) and the support which it received from the Soviet Union – made no change in the nature of Ethiopian colonialism although the degree of repression intensified.

However, even before Eritrea was annexed the armed struggle for liberation had started, and as the years passed the Eritrean people as a whole participated in it. The classes and contradictions created by colonialism pushed the struggle ahead. The workers made redundant when the Ethiopians destroyed and dismantled their factories; the bar-women and domestic servants who faced years of racist treatment and exploitation by the Italians, British and Ethiopians; the poor peasants and nomads living on the edge of starvation whose homes were burnt; and many other groups who made up the Eritrean nation.

In the course of these years the tensions within family structure also increased. The struggle for national liberation heightened them further, first by supporting women fighting oppression within the family and providing them with an alternative to subjugation, and later by actively intervening on their behalf through changes in the laws and political structures of the liberated zone.

In the pages which follow, women who have lived through these remarkable times tell the stories of their communities, their villages, their families and their struggles. As they analyse their lives, they also tell us the story of the Eritrean revolution.[5]

2 Mabrat's Story

"Some people say that women played no part in the early days of our struggle. But it is not true. People think so because only men have written books, written our history. No, women were involved right from the beginning."

Mabrat Kassa's years of political consciousness and activity spanned a long and crucial period in Eritrean history. Sitting in one of the small camouflage huts in Solomona refugee camp in Eritrea's liberated zone where she now lives and works, she talked to us about her life and experiences. Inextricable from these is the story of Eritrea's struggle for freedom.

In her early teens in Asmara she lived through the last bitter days of Italian fascist rule, and it was then that she resolved to fight colonialism. As the years went by she realized that she would also have to face specific and acute oppression as a woman. She was unable to have children, and in Eritrea as in so many other societies this is regarded as an unacceptable shortcoming. It shaped the course of her personal life, but she fought this oppression with dignity and resilience.

"I was born," she told us, "in Mandafera in Serai." And then with uncharacteristic vagueness:

> My age is 50, 55, or maybe 66 years. My father was a judge. He was killed when I was very young. Someone poisoned him, they mixed the bile of an elephant with *suwa* [beer] and made him drink it.... Yes, in those days there were elephants around – even now there are some – and it was not difficult to get the bile.

When I was 13 my mother and elder brother arranged my marriage. And soon after my mother died too. I was never consulted before the marriage was arranged and after my honeymoon I refused to go back to my husband's house. I did not want the marriage, I was too young. My brother was very angry. He threatened to kill me so I ran away. I went to a family who were my father's friends and stayed with them for some time; eventually one of the women took me to live with her sister in Asmara.

That Asmara was very different from the Asmara of today. Where there are houses now there were small vegetable gardens owned by Italian. Gezabanda, now a beautiful residential area, was full of trees and wild fruits which I used to eat.

It was in Asmara that Mabrat experienced the brutality of fascism and colonial rule.

"It was 1935 [this suggests that Mabrat is now nearly seventy]. There were Italian soldiers everywhere and there was a lot of activity because they were preparing for the war [against Ethiopia]. The Italians had gathered a lot of tanks on Ande Mariam [St Mary's Square]. There was high security [and] if an Eritrean passed this area, they would bring their whips and beat them."

It was a time when the Italian regime was at a turning point, not only because it was about to launch a war but because the implications and consequences of this war were enormous. Previously the Italians had exploited Eritrean labour, land and raw materials, shipping minerals, coconut products and other materials to factories in Italy where they were processed and then sold back to Eritrea and neighbouring countries. Now, under fascist dictatorship and after the conquest of Ethiopia, Italy set up a co-ordinated East African Empire consisting of Eritrea, Ethiopia and Somalia. Industries such as petrol, electricity and food processing were now established within the country. Transport networks were set up, including rail and road systems, airports at Asmara and Gura, and expanded port facilities at Massawa and Assab. The cities grew because housing was needed for the vastly increased colonial staff.

Eritrean workers were required for all this, and they poured in from the villages (the population of Asmara increased six-fold between 1935 and 1941). The men were channelled to the most exploitative work in the mines and plantations and to the hardest construction jobs. Of the women some worked in plantations and factories, others faced prostitution in the bars which sprang up to service the colonizers, or worked as domestic servants in their homes. This was the beginning of the Eritrean working class whose struggles 20 years later were the spark which ignited the Eritrean revolution.

Mabrat witnessed this activity and influx of workers. She noticed too the crucial distinction between settler and indigenous labour. "The Italians did not want Eritreans to learn any skilled work. If they saw them doing skilled work they would chase them away." Restricted to a very low level of education, the Eritrean population was denied access to all good jobs. In response to the fascist Italian regime's economic needs: "All trades and occupations were closed [to Eritreans] if they offered employment, however humble, to workers from Italy . . . and . . . the surplus of workers from Italy was so great that Europeans were [sometimes] employed on stone breaking on the roads."[6] This system[7] was justified by Italian writers of the day who argued, for example,[8] that "natives" were employed in the production of cotton, castor-oil seeds, peanuts, coffee and sugar-cane because these crops were either produced in areas climatically unsuitable for Europeans or else required large numbers of workers, exploitative wages for Eritreans keeping profits up in these labour-intensive sectors. The same was true of gold and platinum mines where "it was not possible to think of employing Italian labour for apart from the question of the prestige of the race, [no such enterprise could] bear the wages of European workers".

In the Asmara of Mabrat's youth, the atmosphere and everyday incidents reflected the brutality of this economic system.

There were incidents that happened every day. They used to call us "flies" or "slaves". If they called you *moski* you were supposed to answer. And they called you *fachyanera* [blackface] or *merde* [shit]. There were streets of this city where Eritreans were not allowed – we were not allowed on the main street of Asmara – we had to go on the back streets with the donkeys. And there was one area called "Caserma Mussolini" – if you were found there you could be arrested. And the shops: clothes shops, for example, would be divided into two with a ribbon, one side for Italians and one for Eritreans, with separate entrances. The owners were Yemenis. They would tell you: "this side is for nationals [Italians] and this side is for Eritreans." If the Italians found you on the wrong side they would shout: "Go away, you are *pidocchiose*" [full of lice]. If you answered: "Can't we walk here? Do we have lice even on our legs?" they would say, "Yes, all over!". If an Eritrean was found drunk, the drum would be beaten and everyone would gather. Then they would remove all his clothes except his underpants and give him twenty-five lashes till his skin was broken and peeled.

In this society, the duties of a good Italian colonialist were made quite explicit by the writers of the time:

[We must] make them believe entirely in our absolute, inherent and eternal superiority: we cannot permit ourselves the luxury of revealing our poverty, our preoccupations. . . . The Italian, for the very reason that he is Italian and white, must always and whatever happens be richer than the richest native.[8]

How was this translated into everyday life? Mabrat explained:

Once I had an Italian neighbour who had a restaurant. She used to insult Eritreans: "You are beggars! You are poor! You are black!" I found it unbearable. Then one day an Italian came to my house. He was barefoot and in ragged clothes and he was begging. I asked him where he was from and he said he was from Rome. I took him to the door of my Italian neighbour and knocked. I said, "There's someone here to see you." She was busy in her kitchen trying to make steaks and she came to the door with a double-edged knife. She asked the man where he came from. He said: "Rome". The woman was furious and tried to attack me with the knife. She knew it was my way of showing that it was the Italians who had come to our land, and that there were Italians who were beggars. At that time I was young and strong so she would never have succeeded in injuring me. But the Italian police, the *carabineri*, were called. The told the woman to be careful because Eritreans were very vengeful.

What happened to the Italian beggar? Mabrat did not know. But according to official Italian policy in the mid-1930s, the Italian labourer was to be "treated as a soldier . . . was he not really a soldier? Was he not working for the glory of the Motherland?"[9] In this context begging was a serious offence for which he was probably sent to Assab to "a concentration camp for those few who abandoned their work, were chronically drunk, or showed themselves quarrelsome".

In this period Eritrean women in the cities faced the sexual violence and sexual exploitation characteristic of an apartheid society. Mabrat told us:

> I hated Italian men for the way they behaved. There were many instances of rapes of Eritrean women by Italian men, it was common . . . And it was the Italians who introduced prostitution. In Asmara you could see a lot of prostitutes with red nails and high-heeled shoes but there was a separate area for prostitution. Italians would come and pick women out like any commodity. There was a place called Casino. The owner of this place was an Italian woman and she would go from place to place looking for beautiful women and sometimes forcing them to go with her.

Asmara's Casino was also recalled by other women. Lemlem Hailu from Fishae Merarra village had noticed it on her visits to the city:

> Only prostitutes lived there. They were licensed and checked by doctors. During the Italian period there was a lot of prostitution and also a lot of venereal disease. There were children born with VD. It was the same in Decemhare, there was a place called Casino there too which was a prostitution centre controlled by Italian business.

The relationship between prostitution and colonialism was explained to me by many women. Lemlem, for example, told me: "Colonialism was the cause of prostitution because society was changing but there was no education for women. So if they left home there were no jobs they could go to and there was no other means of survival. Colonialism created prostitution".

All the other women I questioned and the references I could find about prostitution in Eritrea, confirmed the view that prostitution was introduced into Eritrea by colonialism. In Ethiopia, as in many other fully-fledged feudal societies, prostitution is an institution which is openly acknowledged and "accepted" and accessible only to certain classes, but in Eritrea prostitution never formally existed. Being a prostitute in Eritrea is considered much more shameful than it is in Ethiopia. This may be because the notion of shame related to any real or imagined slur on a woman's chastity is strong in Eritrean societies. However, it is more likely to be because in Eritrea prostitution owes its origins to the impact of (colonial) capitalism on an early feudal society. Under capitalism sex is a commodity and prostitution is the ultimate expression of this. Under colonialism it was also accompanied by racism and epitomized powerlessness and degradation. Colonial capitalism, particularly in the fascist period, had instituted deeply hypocritical rules of conduct typical of an apartheid society. As Mabrat commented, no Eritrean man was allowed to have an affair with an Italian woman, it was a criminal offence. Marriages or long-term relationships between Eritrean women and Italian men had been permitted in the early phase of Italian colonialism but were regarded as crimes under the fascist regime, because Eritrean women would influence their husbands in favour of the "natives".

The other type of employment for Eritrean women introduced by colonialism was urban domestic service. In Asmara in the 1930s and 40s it was not only Italians but also rich Eritreans who employed women as domestic servants. Mabrat herself had, at one point, a young girl working for her who "did everything". But the relationship between Eritrean domestic servants and Italian masters and mistresses was different. It was overlaid with racism and was seen by the Eritrean women as a direct result of colonialism. Village families robbed by the colonizers of their best land and impoverished by the breakdown of the rural economy had no choice but to send their sons and daughters into town to seek work.

Hiwet Ogba Georgis, who was later to play such a significant role in the struggle for liberation, described her work first on an Italian planation and then as a domestic servant in Asmara, and spoke of the conditions which forced her to take these jobs:

> My family lived in Debarwa, about 27km from Asmara. I grew up in a *hudmo*. It had one room divided into three part – one for living and sleeping, one part for a kitchen, and one part for the animals. We had a cow and two calves, five goats, a donkey, a dog and an ox. My father was a farmer but we did not have much land. We did not produce enough to see us through the whole year. We used the ox for ploughing but we had only one so we had to join forces with someone else – one day we did our fields and one day theirs. We had milk from the animals and we made butter from it but we did not have enough to sell. After the harvest we sold some grain to buy pepper, oil and so on. . . . When we sold our grain after the harvest we had to sell it very cheap but when we needed to buy it before the next harvest when we did not have any it was very expensive – the price had doubled.
>
> After the harvest my mother would sell some of the crops or my father would sell a goat – that is how we got money to buy clothes. We just had the cheapest clothes and no underclothes. Everything had to be mended all the time and nothing was ever good enough when it was discarded to be handed down to the younger children. We were hungry, especially in the winter. And in the rainy season it was so bad that sometimes we had to go and search for wild vegetables which we might eat. It wasn't so bad during the summer,

at least we usually had some food. Those times were very bad. My whole family were very hungry. My parents never had enough in their lives.

My sister, Amlesset, and I went to work on the plantation after my two older sisters were married. They had been working on the plantation but when they married they moved away to their husbands' villages. The family needed to have someone out working. I was 10 years old and got only 10 pence a day to start with.

I used to scare birds from the tomato crops. Later I went on to picking carrots, cleaning them, packing them and taking them to market. . . . The plantation was owned by Paulino Marasani [whose family was] well known at the time. He started on a small plot and then he expanded; the land he took had once belonged to the people. When I went to work there it was already quite big, with 50 people employed from my village in addition to a large number of seasonal migrant workers. There was never any trouble when I was working there because the owner knew that he could get more labour easily if any of us caused trouble or even complained. It was Amlesset's idea to go to Asmara – she ran away, getting a lift in one of the plantation's lorries. She thought she would try her luck and get a better job and send back more money to our family.

I followed her and eventually (this was about 1950) I started work with an Italian family. It was hard 24 hours a day with only half a day off per week – and it was also degrading. You are never called by your name, only "*Letai*" [servant] and they insult you as "dirty!" or "black!" The food you are given is entirely different from what your employers eat. Even the bread is of two kinds – white for them and brown for us. We had to wear uniform and cover our hair all the time. In fact we were not allowed to take care of our hair in the house. We had to get permission to go out and oil it.

All domestic workers were afraid of being sexually attacked – that is why we always preferred houses with old people or with a lot of children. Italian men would rape domestic workers and if they got pregnant they would kick them out and deny any connection with them.[11]

Employment as bar-women and domestic servants symbolized the exploitation and suffering faced by Eritrean women in urban areas of colonized Eritrea. Their oppressed position was further emphasised by almost all interactions with the colonizers and their agents. For example, Mabrat remembered one occasion when an Italian man in a car had run over an Eritrean woman and killed her.

> He just smashed her body. I do not know if it was deliberate. Then the Italians beat a drum, they did this whenever they wanted to call us. We went there and found the woman lying dead. They asked us to identify her. Then I saw that they had put a 30-franc coin on her mouth. I called a man who I knew was an Eritrean spy working for the Italians. I asked him the meaning of this. He said: "That is her worth." I said: "Are we worth only 30 francs? Is that what our life is worth?" The man said: "Shut up! You are too young to understand."

By 1936, the woman she was living with had arranged another marriage for Mabrat. This time she had been consulted and she had agreed. "My second husband," she told us, "was a driver employed by rich Eritreans and drivers were well thought of at the time. I liked him . . . he used to bring a lot of butter, a lot of cereals . . . it was a life of luxury." As a comfortably well-off young housewife in Asmara, acutely aware of her surroundings, Mabrat was in an ideal position to watch all the changes in this history city. She saw the war against Ethiopia, with massive forced conscription from the rural areas. The Italian victory brought in its wake a new alliance with England and France, who abandoned their old ally Haile Selassie and officially recognized Ethiopia as an Italian colony. Scarcely six years later the Second World War started, and Italy was defeated by the same Western Allies.

With the colonizers defeated, Asmara, like Eritrea itself, was facing a new political phase full of tension and uncertainty. Would the Eritrean people now achieve self-determination? This question was being asked by a section of the Eritrean population, including the liberal intelligentsia. But the British became the new colonizers; they declared Eritrea (and also Ethiopia) an occupied enemy territory. A military administration was set up, based on the Hague Convention of 1907[3] which gave the occupier the right to redirect the assets of an occupied territory to its own war efforts, while at the same time declaring that humane principles "do not apply to uncivilised states and tribes". British racism and brutality were in a class of their own. As Mabrat put it: "The Italians would give their leftovers to us, but the British would simply throw them away. They would break their bottles, make holes in their bear cans." Where the Italians had been brutal, the British with their aloof arrogance were inhuman – because while the Italians wanted to present themselves as superior ("We must not reveal our poverty . . ."), the British colonialist really believed in their own superiority.

The aims of the British Military Administration were: to ensure the security of the occupying forces; to ensure the preservation of peace and good order; and to ensure the exploitation of the economic resources of the territory.[10] At the same time it would "undertake the direct administration of the country with little assistance from the government machines of the former administration or from the chiefs of the indigenous population". Britain and her allies used Eritrea to the utmost to meet their wartime needs. Two hospitals were established and a garage was set up to repair planes; a naval base was built in Massawa by the Americans; and port facilities were repaired and expanded. All this helped to boost the economy. Italian-owned factories were reopened and since basic commodities could not be imported, because of the war, many light industries were set up to meet the day-to-day needs of the Europeans and the new Eritrean middle classes.

At the same time, Eritrea remained in effect an Italian colony and Italians continued to play an important role in the economy. Not only did Crown land continue to belong to the State and rich Italians, but Italian control over land in the rural areas increased in this period: when the British had to dispose of extra land they would almost invariably allocate it to Italians who were described as those "best qualified and equipped to use it". Because of this there were many struggles over land, the peasants taking on both the feudal upper classes and the rich Italian farmers.

According to Mabrat, at this time Asmara was a city of edgy chaos. Soldiers from different parts of the world were brought in by the British – Indians, Sudanese and others. They were everywhere: guarding the fortress in Asmara, for example. There were also ex-soldiers, Eritreans previously conscripted into the defeated Italian army who now poured into the towns.

Against this background there had developed a variety of political forces. First, the Party of Love of Country (PLC) was set up, mainly by Eritrean intellectuals from rural backgrounds with western liberal aspirations, and led, among others, by the charismatic Wolde-Ab Wolde-Mariam who was to play a historic role in the future struggle of Eritrea. The PLC opposed the Ethiopian feudal state and also the traditional social order in the country, but because it represented an essentially petit bourgeois nationalism it was unable to create a national (rather than a regional) identity. Despite this, however, it did frighten the Ethiopians. They began to oppose it by whipping up anti-Muslim sentiments (the PLC stressed Christian – Muslim unity). Later, after the decolonization of Ethiopia in 1944, the Ethiopian state set up the Society for the Unification of Eritrea and Ethiopia (SUEE) specifically to combat the PLC. The SUEE consisted of Eritrean employees of the Ethiopian state. They used both infiltration and agitation in their attempts to discredit the British and Italians, while at the same time opposing, infiltrating and finally splitting the PLC.

Throughout this period, according to Mabrat:

> The British were also creating conflict among the people. . . . In Eritrea, Christian and Muslim, we have come from the same ancestors. Sometimes there are Christian and Muslim families with close relations, but the British succeeded in dividing us. . . . There were two officers in the administration, Cooper and Brazi, who were well-known for doing this. . . . They created conflict between a lot of different groups, for example between the Geberti [Tigrinya-speaking Muslims] and Jebelli [people originally from

Yemen]. The Geberti began shouting for the Jebelli to leave their country. The Jebelli view was that we have been brought up here, we work here and live here, this is our place. They fought with sticks and stones in a place called Gezebrahan.

Although the divide-and-rule principle worked at all levels, according to Mabrat it was the two largest groups, the Muslims and Christians, which the British most wanted to set against each other. On 26 August 1946, the tensions which had been created exploded into violence in what has come to be known as the Sudan Defense Force (SDF) Incident. Mabrat described it as follows:

> Some Sudanese soldiers and Eritreans were playing cards. The Sudanese won but the Christians demanded their money back. They beat up, some say killed a Sudanese. Then Cooper brought more Sudanese soldiers and said: "Christians have killed your brothers." These soldiers were heavily armed . . . they went from house to house killing, shooting, shouting: "Are you a Christian or a Muslim?" One Sudanese sergeant killed every Christian in his path. Cooper watched all this without a word. . . . All this was done to keep Christians and Muslims busy fighting each other – to prevent them from getting together to fight for freedom.

Gebre-Medhin quotes British Military Administration figures of the dead and injured in this incident: 40 Copts killed and 64 injured, 2 Eritrean Muslims killed and 10 injured, and 3 SDF soldiers killed and 13 injured. He notes that these figures are probably suspect and infers from the SDF casualties that there were other armed parties involved, probably Ethiopians.[10]

The SDF Incident was followed by a major attempt to resolve the differences within the PLC, which by now had split into two main factions at a Waala (meeting). Gebre-Medhin writes:

> The genius behind the idea of the Waala . . . Ato Wolde-Ab Wolde-Mariam, editor of the *Eritrean Weekly News* . . . was a well-known advocate of Eritrean independence. Concerned by the erosion of PLC unity, the ongoing religious and regional crisis in Eritrean society, and the role the Ethiopian state was playing to destabilise the Eritrean political economy, Ato Wolde-Ab approached the

pro-Ethiopian PLC faction, to open a dialogue between the two PLC groupings with the hope of establishing a united front. . . . The planning of the Waala had thus begun.[10]

However, as soon as the Ethiopian state became aware of the plans it intervened, even before the day of the meeting, and the agreements already reached were nullified.

The Waala of November 1946 was a milestone in Eritrean politics because it represented the most direct Ethiopian intervention so far; saw the formation of the pro-Ethiopian Unionist Party supported by the traditional nobility, merchants from Massawa and the Eritrean Coptic Church; and saw the final collapse of the PLC. It led almost immediately to the emergence of a number of new parties: the Muslim League, the Pro-Italian Party, the National Muslim Party of Massawa and others which eventually formed the independence bloc. The bloc was opposed to Ethiopian rule and supported a gradual move towards independence under the auspices of the United Nations (UN). In Asmara the tension and violence continued. The British played an active role in this; they were now advocating the partitioning of Eritrea, with Sudan getting the Muslim west and Ethiopia the Christian south.

Eventually, with France, Britain, the United States and the Soviet Union unable to agree, a UN commission comprising representatives from Norway, South Africa, Burma, Pakistan and Guatemala was set up to help decide the future of Eritrea. The commission visited Eritrea for two months in early 1950. Its brief was "to consider the wishes and welfare of the inhabitants of Eritrea . . . the capacity of the people for self government . . . the interests of peace and security in East Africa . . . and the rights and claims of Ethiopia including in particular Ethiopia's legitimate need for adequate access to the sea". It carried out what one British observer described as "casual observations of rival political gatherings . . . random questions to persons whose representative qualities it had no means of checking".[12] Underlying the commission's task were the wishes of the US government, expressed in 1952 by the US Secretary of State, John Foster Dulles:

> From the point of view of justice, the opinions of the Eritrean people must receive consideration. Nevertheless the strategic interests of the United States in the Red Sea basin and considerations of security and world peace make it necessary that the country has to be linked with our ally Ethiopia.

The UN commission did not come up with unanimous recommendations but the majority of its members, Norway, South Africa and Burma, were in favour of federation with Ethiopia. The December 1950 UN General Assembly accepted this majority decision and recommended that Eritrea become an autonomous unit with its own "legislative, executive, and judicial powers in the field of domestic affairs but federated with Ethiopia under the sovereignty of the Ethiopian crown". But as Gebre-Medhin has pointed out,[10] because of the absolutist and authoritarian nature of the Ethiopian state, such a federation was a contradiction in terms. The Ethiopian imperial state could never have allowed it to exist because it would pose a threat to its own continuance.

In Mabrat's personal life the years just before Federation brought an intensely painful realization – that she was unable to have children. In Eritrean society this is a terrible failing for a woman. She went to see Dr Vero, a gynaecologist whom she mentioned to us not in this context but while discussing Italian racism:

> Dr Vero was a gynaecologist but when women went to see him for whatever gynaecological problem he would perform a hysterectomy. He would do it under anaesthetic without telling them in advance. Women go mad after that, I had that experience. It has happened to a lot of women. After the operation we have no menstruation, nothing. It was deliberately done to decrease the population of Eritrea – there was nothing the Italians did not do.

Soon after this her marriage broke up. To be divorced for failing to producing a child is a terrible blow, but with typical restraint Mabrat hardly mentioned her feelings, saying only: "We had been together for 15 years . . . he divorced me because I had not had a child . . ."

Despite the pain of her divorce, at least Mabrat was not destitute, nor did she become dependent on her brother as many women of a lower class would have done. After all, she was the daughter of a judge and as such was part of the richest strata of rural society. In addition she was a strong, capable woman conscious of her rights. She told us:

> After my divorce I got my share of our savings. Out of my share ... I bought a house for 17,000 Ethiopian dollars and I still had enough left to employ a servant to clean and cook – in those days labour was cheap. I lived on my own quite happily for some time but people started saying: "You can't live alone, you must get married again!" So I told them: "I can't have children so there is no point," but they insisted. In the end I gave in to them and got married again. My new husband was a farmer. His land was in the outlying area of Asmara, but farming alone was not enough to produce a comfortable livelihood and he also made some money by repairing things for the Italians. Later he had a job in a glass factory ...

Mabrat's parents-in-law had a separate house, as is often the case in Eritrean urban extended families, but: "They spent most of their time in our house. During the early days of my marriage I can remember everyone in Asmara was crying out: "My country! My country!"

With her growing political consciousness, Mabrat had begun to relate everything important in her life to the historic events of the Eritrean struggle. This was during the first half of the 1950s, a period of intense political activity particularly in Asmara. "Federation" brought with it not the principles of federalism but the Ethiopian army of occupation and a variety of repressive laws. Eritrean languages were replaced by Amharic. Amharic even became the language of the courts. Basic democratic rights such as freedom of expression were eroded. The federal flag was imposed. Books in Tigrinya were collected and burnt, and people involved in peaceful protest were subjected to imprisonment and torture. As Mabrat put it: "People became involved because their day-to-day life was affected. Ethiopian oppression created consciousness in every household."

The people of Eritrea resisted, this time through mass organizations of workers, students and the self-employed. They fought colonialism using strikes and boycotts. For Mabrat, this was the political turning-point when the struggle really started. It was the same for many others of all ages. People like Ande Michael Kahsai (now a Central Committee member of the EPLF) recall that period too:

> I was 14 and in the sixth grade when we had our first Amharic class. By then Wolde-Ab was broadcasting from Cairo. You could hear the grown-ups talking about it. We did not have a radio at home, but in the tea-shops and so on, people listened to Wolde-Ab. At that time we did not even speak Amharic. One day this Ethiopian teacher came to our class. Eritrean teachers at that time had a starting salary the equivalent of $20, later it became $80, whereas the starting salary of the Ethiopian teachers was $250, because all the revenues from the port and so on from Eritrea were going to the Ethiopian Federal Government. So our Eritrean teachers were dressed in khaki, the same khaki they wear the year through. But this teacher came in a three-piece suit and a neck tie. It made quite an impression. Of course he was not simply a teacher who came to teach language but an intelligence officer responsible for indoctrination. He went to the black-board and wrote "Haile Selassie" on one side and "Wolde-Ab Wolde Mariam" on the other. This was the first Amharic class and he asked:, "Who is better?" One of our classmates stood up and said: "Wolde-Ab is better", so a kind of confrontation was created. It was unconscious resistance but it was there.
>
> When we went to high school in 1959, there was resistance to Amharic in our group. Our favourite method was to eat dried chick-peas during the class. It was very noisy. We were known as the chick-pea market. We were notorious! . . . In 1958 there were all the demonstrations and strikes in Asmara. We were not fully informed but we went in solidarity.

A considerable number of women students were involved in these strikes and demonstrations, but unlike their male comrades they were in general not arrested. According to Worku Zerai of the National Union of Eritrean Women, this could have been because:

In the 1950s there were Eritrean police and guards and they did not mistreat women in the same way as the Ethiopians were to do later. Actually the policemen were in a dilemma because when the Eritrean students sang patriotic songs, the policemen identified with them. But they attacked demonstrators with tear gas. They did not want to arrest women and they would say to them: "You go home, you are women." But the women refused to leave their male comrades.

Central to the political activity of the period was the Workers' Syndicate, a unique combination of trade union and anti-colonial organization, set up by Wolde-Ab Wolde Mariam among others. It organized demonstrations and sustained the General Strike of 1958 in which an overwhelming proportion of Eritrean workers united to challenge the government over the dismantling of Eritrean status. The strike held out for three days, paralysing the government. Then it was crushed with unprecedented brutality, when the army was ordered to open fire. Hundreds of workers were killed and injured, and the Workers' Syndicate was banned. The incident, has been described as the Sharpeville of Eritrea, and it led to more intense, and now revolutionary, political activity.

The clandestine Group of Seven, Eritrea's first revolutionary nationalist organization, was set up in late 1958. Such was the mood of anger and resistance that large numbers of people, particularly young people, wanted to be involved in the Group of Seven. As Ande Michael said: "Some of us were members. We did not know what we wanted, other than Eritrean independence. Our main activity was distributing leaflets. Some were signed by Wolde-Ab. I don't know if they were authentic." The Ethiopian state then broadened its attack upon the Eritrean working class. It adopted the strategy of "drying the pond to catch the fish". Factories were dismantled and transferred to Addis Ababa, weakening the Eritrean economy while at the same time undermining the trade unions. But nothing could weaken the intense nationalism which had been aroused in the late 1950s. In 1961 the Eritrean Liberation Front (ELF) was formed, and it launched the armed struggle for liberation (see Chapter 3). A year later the Ethiopian state annexed Eritrea. While obviously achieved through intimidation and deceit (armed police were present in parliament and military units formed blocades outside), the annexation was presented as officially sanctioned by the Eritrean parliament.

Mabrat told of these major developments in Eritrean politics only in passing – they were important milestones in Eritrean history, but not ones she wished to dwell upon. In those years she had been isolated from the outside world by the intense suffering of another divorce. This time it was her parents-in-law who were responsible because, as in many traditional marriages, it was they and not the husband or wife who took the decisions which mattered.

> After 13 or 14 years of marriage my parents-in-law started putting pressure on him to divorce me because I had not had a child . . . In the end, while I was still married to him they got him engaged to someone else. After that I thought that it was better to get divorced. After the divorce I hated being in the same area. I rented a house in another part of the city and moved there . . .

Optimistic and resilient as always, however, Mabrat soon recovered. She found a job for herself. "Really it was a sort of catering business. Haile Selassie's daughter was funding students to become priests and I provided their meals. I employed a servant to make *injeera* [a type of pancake which is a staple in Eritrean cooking] and sauce and I managed the whole thing myself." These student priests, directly financed by the imperial state, represented a characteristic aspect of the Haile Selassie regime: its feudal social relations, its attempt to take control of popular ideology in Eritrea by controlling the Church, and its obsession with ritualized personal power for the emperor.

There was also another face of the Haile Selassie regime which was apparent in Asmara: the neocolonial reality which was interwoven with these feudal social relations. And Eritrea, as the colony of a neocolony, experienced imperialist exploitation even more directly than the rest of Ethiopia. In 1953, a US telecommunications centre was set up in south-west Asmara:

an early indication of Haile Selassie's concern for US "security". By the 1960s this had expanded to a military base, the Kagnew station. The farmland required for the base was confiscated from the peasants. Those who resisted were simply shot dead. While all Eritreans were excluded from the base except for a few servants and those with jobs such as receptionists there (even the guards were American), the presence of American soldiers had an impact on the city itself. Bars and discos were springing up in large numbers, and as one upper middle-class woman, then in her teens, described it:

> There were all kinds of special shops and duty-frees and certainly in the early sixties it was fashionable to have an American boyfriend. Just think of it, 3,000 US soldiers and many of them single men – more than anything it encouraged prostitution. Quite a few Americans took Eritrean women back as wives – many of them had been prostitutes.

Eritrean urban culture was not deeply affected, however. Increased prostitution invariably increases the control which society exerts over "good" and "pure" women. Changes in the position of women were therefore mainly external and cosmetic, while essentially feudal relations and values were preserved. In fact these values and relations were merely adjusted to capitalist society, while preserving the same ideology, the same attitude to women, and on the whole even the same rules. In some cases the changes intensified women's oppression: for example, dowries went up (and they were to rise even more sharply as time went by; see Chapter 7). Davit Hailemariam described her elder sister's marriage in Asmara in 1962:

> The first daughter has to have a big traditional marriage. Ever since she was 12 or 13 years old, families would approach us for my sister but she didn't want to get married. Finally when she was in the sixth grade, they forced her. The man has to be from the right area and of course the right class. He can be blind or crippled or handsome, it does not matter. The woman? Everything depends on her, what kind of kids she is going to give, her dowry, how tall she is, how beautiful she is. The surprising thing was that my sister's husband

was a teacher in the same school, but he could not ask her. His family sent a delegate, a man – it is always a man. The mother may be the one who has actually chosen the girl for her son, but she tells her husband and he approaches the elders of the area and they send someone. If the girl does not like him, she has to give a solid reason, and she tells her mother who tells her father. My sister was bound by this culture, but also once she was engaged she had to have no contact at all with her fiance. If he appeared she had to run away. We were the go-betweens passing secret love-letters. And once my sister even managed to go and see a movie with him without anyone knowing. But she did not want to marry, and she said to my father: "Why are you doing this to me?" In the end a condition was made that after marriage she would be allowed to finish school. That was in 1962, and she managed to finish school. Now she has seven kids – they are still in Asmara – a middle-class family.

However, the late 1950s and early 1960s were in a sense the end of an era, because after that the effects of the struggle for freedom were to reach out and dramatically change people's lives and futures. Davit herself was to escape this type of marriage mainly because of intense political activity in Asmara in the mid-1970s when she reached a marriageable age (see Chapter 4).

In an atmosphere where women's dependence on men had to be seen to be complete (even if in reality it was not), Mabrat's situation as a divorced, childless woman living quite contentedly and successfully on her own was simply unacceptable. If she had been a depressed widow dependent on her relatives no one would have bothered her, except perhaps to try to exploit her sexually. But Mabrat was not depressed or discontented. In Eritrea, as in most other capitalist and semi-feudal societies which strive to control women's sexuality, self-sufficiency on the part of a woman not yet middle-aged causes both bafflement and unease. So despite all the suffering she had been through, friends, relatives and even the Church began to pressurize Mabrat to marry again.

> I was living quite happily on my own when the friends of a man called Phasame approached me. They told me that his wife had left

him and gone off to Addis leaving three children – would I please marry him and help him raise the three children? I said: "I can't have children, and I don't want a husband." But he brought priests and elders to beg me. "Please help him," they said. I told them that I was living a good life and did not want him, but in the end I agreed.

He was a teacher and soon after we were married he was transferred to Massawa, so I went too. Massawa was dominated by the naval base – the Ethiopian navy in this period! [the early 1960s]. What was it like for women? Well, for a woman looking for work there was not much choice. There were prostitutes, and there were women working as domestics in the naval base with Ethiopian families and some working with Eritrean families. Some were working in soft-drinks factories and very, very few were working in offices. But most women were housewives like me. My husband had a lot of guests and we used to buy *suwa* so in the end we decided to make a *suwa* house with the licence in my name. It was a tremendous success. We became very rich and bought a lot of houses, 28 in all. We became very popular in Massawa and our name became well known among the rich and the well established.

It was perhaps inevitable that Mabrat should now become more closely involved with the struggle she had identified with and tried to observe for so long. The incidents that led to her being drawn into it are typical of her class and position in Massawa:

One of the people who would come to our *suwa* house was Ibrahim Terafic, a cousin of Othman Sabe, the ex-ELF leader. Sometimes I would see him talking to people and noting their names. I would ask him: "Why do you register people?" and he would reply: "I am looking for people to work on my farm." But I found out that he was in fact recruiting people for the "Group of Seven" movement; he was forming cells in my house. I told him that I knew his story. I told him: "You are doing things that affect every Eritrean, you should have involved me too." I became a member and gave him a separate room for meetings. My husband did not know about it, he thought they came to drink *suwa*.

Before long I once again had to face problems with my marriage. My husband's first wife found out that he had become rich and successful, and at the same time she had a quarrel with her brother in Addis. So one day the brother turned up in Massawa and told me to leave his sister's house. Then he came again and threatened me with a pistol. He went back to Massawa but in the meantime I got ill and had to go to hospital in Asmara. It was while I was in hospital that his first wife came back and started her life again with her husband. When I returned I found her there. I could see that the man hated to see me back. He told me to leave.

I had come back to Massawa on a Sunday evening and on Monday we got divorced. I took my belongings, and our property was shared in half. He took 14 houses and I got 14. I also had plenty of gold ornaments and a lot of money. I continued with my *suwa* business in Massawa and became, if anything, even more rich and popular. And I continued my activities with the Group of Seven. I would take appointments for people who wanted to see Ibrahim Terafic, I would hide people and find out information.

In the early 1960s the activities of the Group were reaching a peak. Based on cells of seven people, the organization was increasingly co-ordinating its urban guerrilla operations with the ELF which was beginning to take the Ethiopian army on in the lowlands. By all accounts the Group did not have a large number of women members, but there were a few very active ones. Gedey Fassaha "Gandhi" was one of them. The daughter of "Gandhi" who acted in these crucial years as a political deputy to Wolde-Ab, Gedey was aware of her father fighting for independence in the late 1940s. She too remembers the mid-1950s as the point when the struggle started. Married at the age of 13 in 1955, she and her husband became involved in the Group of Seven in 1961.

> We used to agitate, carry out operations and after 1963 when we established a connection with the field, we used to collect money for the struggle. In March 1966 on Ethiopian New Year we carried out an operation in Asmara near the fuel-station. My husband was involved in this. The Ethiopians found out about it. An infiltrator in the group had given information to the police. At that point we had in our house two machine guns and about one thousand bullets; we had kept them there for about eight months and I was the one

responsible for them. I remember the speed with which we acted: we got hold of a car, took them to the house of the infiltrator and put them under his bed. He was out and his mother was blind so she could not see. Three hours later the police raided our house. One of the comrades responsible for that operation escaped to the front, and six others were arrested. To start with they were all given death sentences but later these were changed to sentences of 13, 7, and 4 years. My husband and two others were fined and placed under house arrest. That was my husband's third arrest; the first time he had been tortured.

After 1966-7 the Group of Seven was finished. At that time there were very few Eritrean women fighters. In my husband and I we decided that one of us should look after the kids and one should go to the field. Of course we both wanted to go to the field so we drew lots. I won. But my husband escaped early the next morning. He joined the EPLF [Eritrean People's Liberation Front], his friends had convinced him, but I stayed in the ELF. I joined the EPLF in 1980.

When the Group of Seven collapsed Mabrat's image of apolitical prosperity enabled her to play a crucial role:

The Ethiopians started doing house-to-house searches. I hid quite a few people at that time, it was a risk but we guessed that the Ethiopians would not search my house. They just did not suspect me. Eventually the people I was hiding left and for a while I lost contact with the fighters . . . but then the struggle started again. . . . Once again I allowed the ELF to use my house and when the EPLF emerged I started working with the fighters who came from the field – this was between 1975 and 1977. I used to hide them in my house but I also fed them with information. They asked me to do specific tasks: for example, to study the people who were to be assassinated. On one occasion the Ethiopians arrested 68 people in one night and killed them all. They were obviously using spies. I studied the case and found out who the informers were. I told the fighters and they took steps.

I was very close to the Ethiopians so they never suspected me. Actually they like me so much that when they formed the Keble, the administration of Massawa, they made me the chair. At first I refused but the EPLF asked me to accept the office. So I became the chairwoman and began to feed the EPLF with information. Once, in 1976, two EPLF fighters came running to my house. They had just done an operation: they had just burnt down an important building. They said: "Save us! It is up to you to save us!" I said: "I'll try, if I die I'll die with you." I hid them in my house, and the Ethiopians started searching from house to house. When I saw them coming near my house, I rushed out crying and covering my face with a scarf. They asked me what was wrong. I said: "These bastards have burnt our place! They have destroyed our revolutionary state!" When the EPLF attacked Massawa I told them where they could find the money of the Keble and they took it.

In December 1977 the EPLF attacked Massawa. People were leaving the town and Mabrat left also. "At that point it looked as though Massawa was about to be taken by the EPLF so we all stayed in the rural areas nearby, but soon this became unsafe so we had to move further away and eventually went to Ghinda." Mabrat was by now in her late fifties. She had left all her considerable belongings behind in Massawa but she mentioned it only in passing:

Ghinda was the place where the food for the fighters in the battle of Massawa was being prepared. It needed to be carefully organized and I became one of the organizers. I had left everything behind. I started my life afresh with the fighters . . . Ghinda was full of Ethiopian spies, and while I was there I exposed two groups of them. Later, during the strategic withdrawal I came to Sahel with others from Ghinda. There too I worked making sanitary towels (they were made manually before we got the machine). . . . And I still work, helping fighters. I had asked to be registered in the militia but they refused. In the last few years I have been living and working here in the Solomona camp.

3 Laying the Foundations

For women, since they are rarely the founders or acknowledged leaders of liberation struggles, the acid test for any liberation movement is its approach to and record on democracy and people's participation. But since the emergence of a liberation movement itself is a historical process – in this case as in many others the product of a semi-feudal colonial society – the creation of a movement which is democratic in its internal structure, as well as its approach to the population it represents, requires a major struggle in itself. In Eritrea this struggle consisted of the long and often bitter political and finally military confrontations which saw their most acute phase in the years from 1967 to 1974. The political struggles occurred within the Eritrean Liberation Front (ELF), the first liberation movement to emerge. The culmination of these struggles led to the formation of the Eritrean People's Liberation Front (EPLF), and this was followed by civil war within the Eritrean nation.

To understand this period in the history of Eritrea I sought women who had not only lived through it and participated in it, but whose oppression as women was central to their perception of it. One of them is "Adei" (mother) Ogba Habte. I saw her first on my visit to Heshkep, the EPLF administrative centre, on a night when two EPLF cadres were getting married. They were from different ethnic nationalities. About a hundred and fifty people were gathered to witness the simple ceremony. I remember the ullulation, the smiles, the *suwa*, the paper flowers and the atmosphere charged with mixed feelings: celebration and restraint, and a longing for the restraint to be over. Like so much else in Eritrea, the simplicity of the event itself was curiously moving. On the dais were the bride, the groom, and Askalu Menkarios who was officiating for the EPLF. There were also two older women in traditional dress, and a man; they were not parents but respected friends. Later there was dancing, with a special wedding dance in which the couple danced under a canopy of scarves carried by their friends.

Early in the morning we returned to the scene to find it unrecognizably different. I realized that the wedding reception had been held on part of a path leading to one of the semi-camouflaged buildings, and had all been cleared away. We sought out one of the older women who had been on the dais and asked if we might speak with her. She led us to another building which was part of the Public Administration Department and we found an empty room. Could she tell us her life story? She laughed in surprise and then, clasping her cheek, she said:

> I have always wanted to tell my story. Now at last someone has asked me, I am so happy! My name is "Adei" Ogba Habte, and I am from Meretasevene village – that is where I was brought up. And before that – originally – I come from Tzenadegle village in the area south of the Asmara – Massawa road. My age is around fifty.

She spoke slowly and, according to Worku who as so often was interpreting for me, rather ramblingly. But for me her story was crucial. It helped me to understand some central aspects of women's oppression, personal struggles and identity in the eyes of society. It also gave me a glimpse of the experiences of the masses in that period of history when the correct strategy, armed struggle, had been found but when the vehicle to push it forward had not yet been perfected.

In Mabrat's narrative we saw how the story of Eritrea's struggle for liberation was beginning to unfold. First, in the period 1941–52, nationalism was becoming a strong political force and organizing was on the increase but there was still no national organization with a clear direction. There followed a distinct phase during 1952–61 when this political force increased and new organizations emerged, culminating in the formation of the Group of Seven (or the Eritrean Liberation Movement (ELM) as it was called outside the country). This period saw a change in strategy with the realization that open, peaceful protest was not enough and a gradual acceptance that armed struggle was necessary. It was in this period that "political struggles . . . not only created favourable conditions for the formation of a single national struggle but trained what could be the core of a liberation movement".[13]

With the Eritrean people prepared for full-scale armed struggle one might have expected the ELM to launch it; instead it was the Eritrean Liberation Front (ELF), an organization very different in its ideology and its original mass base, which took the initiative and secured leadership of the armed struggle. Looking back at this period the Eritrean People's Liberation Front (EPLF) examines why this happened:

> Why was it the ELF and not the ELM that launched the armed struggle in 1961? Was it because the ELM lacked the preparedness or the will? or was it that a line more progressive than the ELM was required and the ELF supplied it? In other words was there a historical necessity for the ELF? The inception of the armed struggle in 1961 was undeniably the expression of the aspirations of the Eritrean people for independence. Hence its historical importance. The advent of the ELF as the leader of the armed struggle, however, was purely a historical accident.[13]

The leaders of the ELF were people who had left Eritrea during the political upheavals of the 1940s and 1950s, exiled mainly in the Middle East. They had been strongly influenced by the bitter, highly divisive politics of the 1940s, but less so by events in the period immediately following it in the federation with Ethiopia. During the latter time the struggles of the Eritrean working class and the emergence of the Group of Seven had for the first time forged a strong national consciousness in urban centres. The ELF leaders had seen how the Party of Love of Country (PLC) had been transformed into the Unionist Party through the intervention of the Ethiopian church and the infiltration of the Ethiopian government, and how Muslim leaders denied a voice had set up the Muslim League. In this period, while the two political camps were not strictly segregated along religious lines – many Christian leaders allied themselves with the Muslim League and many Muslim chiefs (*diglals*) joined the Unionists – the atmosphere had been charged with tensions between Muslims and Christians, and this was perhaps uppermost in their minds because it was their last experience in Eritrea. They had little or no involvement in the more progressive struggles which emerged from this period, such as the massive trade union strikes, and they had not borne the brunt of the unprecedented repression with which the Ethiopian state responded.

Their actions and strategies also suggest that they did nothing to reject the attitudes and sentiments which had grown first as a result of their traditional semi-feudal culture, and second out of their bitter experiences in the politics of the 1940s. This had implications not only in their approach to different religious and ethnic groups in Eritrea but, as we shall see, in their attitude to women.

Despite all this, however, it was the ELF which carried the struggle forward into the next crucial stage, the armed struggle. It launched its first operations in an ideal arena, the remote Western lowlands bordering Sudan and the Red Sea. The Ethiopians responded in their now traditional way, with reprisals against the civilian population. By 1963 there were more than 3,000 civilians in prison merely on suspicion of helping the ELF. In the rural areas when villages were suspected of harbouring ELF fighters they would simply be destroyed and their inhabitants killed or else ordered to leave.

But let us return to Addai Ogba and her experience of both the ELF and the Ethiopians, intermingled with the parallel story of her personal life.

> My father was a farmer. My mother was a housewife but as a housewife you don't do only housework, you look after the cows and goats. My parents arranged my marriage at the age of 16. Partly it was because they wanted me to stay on with them, but also because we were a Catholic family and among Catholics marriage is not allowed if you are under 15. They say that if you are married

before 15 then it is not a marriage between two people but between "bread and drink".

My married life – there is none that I can talk about. After I finished my honeymoon I went to the lowlands to stay with a family who were friends of my family. They were Gebertis. The man sold firewood. In their house, one day when I was on my own, I was forced, raped by a friend of the Geberti man. He also was a Muslim . . .

When I was pregnant I used to say to my sister: "When I give birth you must throw my child away." But things do not go the way you plan them – things can be beyond your control. After I gave birth they put him in a small bed. He was very beautiful. His hair was down to his eyes, his eyes were very beautiful. I told my sister I had changed my mind. She was happy too. She started playing with the baby.

But my father continued to be very angry. He would tell my mother: "You should make that child eat cow dung and kill him – it is a shame to raise the son of a Muslim." My mother said: "Alright, we can kill the baby but who is going to answer in heaven?" If I had the consciousness then which I have now I would have run away with my child but my life had been so tied up with cows and goats, my mentality was like them.

It was in those days that I developed my addiction to coffee, because when my father came I used to run away and go to my mother, and she used to give me coffee.

When my child was 3 or 4, men started coming to my house and asking for my hand. But I always refused, I did not want to marry a Christian. It made my father very angry, and he would say: "How long do you want to go on like this? Do you want to become a prostitute?" In the end he insisted that I got married. At Easter I was married to a man who lived in Demas and within a week there was trouble. I gave my husband a glass of milk, and he tasted it strangely so I asked him why. He said: "I wanted to see if it was yoghurt." I asked him why, and he said: "I saved you when you disgraced yourself. I saved you, how can you doubt me?" I was very angry. When he left I closed the house and went home to my parents. My father was sitting there with three other men. I said: "You forced me to marry. I said I would never marry a Christian and now I have come back." But they would not listen, they forced me to go back to my husband.

After three or four months he again started insulting me: "I am a son of lords, I married you who have been used by Muslims." Again I went back to my parents and was forced to go back to my husband.

My life was very hard – quarrelling with my husband, leaving him and then being forced to go back. Then I became pregnant and gave birth to a girl. The insults continued – not only from my husband but from others. I would be with a group of women and then just as I was leaving I would hear them say: "this is a woman who has a child by a Muslim", or "you know that beautiful child – his father is a Muslim". I would hear the in-laws say I was a disgrace to the family because Muslims had played with me. I had another baby – another girl. My parents-in-law should have been delighted because my husband had been married four times before and had never succeeded in having children, but instead all they could say was: "It is a child from a Muslim woman." (Yes, if a Muslim sleeps with you you become a Muslim!)

At that time [if Ogba was about 50 at the time of the interview, this must have been around 1964] the ELF were roaming around the villages, demanding food and forcing the villagers to bring them food. Sometimes I also would accept this identity of a Muslim and be happy that the ELF who were known as Muslims were terrorizing the Christian villagers. Often my husband would insult me and then say: "I better be careful because your brothers are governing so you might put me in trouble." One night when he was talking this way the ELF came into the house and I told them I wanted a divorce. I did not like to do it this way but I had no choice. They took me aside and one of them told me that they would take my husband to prison. Then they made an appointment to see him again! But before the date of the appointment, the Ethiopians came and destroyed the whole village.

Two months previously they had destroyed two other villages and killed everyone who lived in them, and they had come to Demas straight from there, so we were afraid that they would kill all of us too. The Amharas asked us to gather under a bridge. People left all their belongings and begged the Amharas for their lives. Our lives were spared but we lost everything. The Ethiopians made a military camp in our village and all of us had to leave. The Arabs in the village went to their country. Of the rest some of us went to Ginda, some to Massawa. My husband went to the highlands. I went with a Sudanese man to Massawa. I had nothing except the hammock to carry my children on my back. When we got there I just put some papers down on the floor and slept.

The Ethiopians finished our married life so that problem was over. In Massawa the Sudanese man and I were together. One day a woman of the Saho nationality from Demas came across me and my children. She asked me why I was there and I told her our village had been destroyed. She brought me a quintal of flour, a water container and some blankets. That is what made it possible for me to survive; also I would make a little money by plaiting women's hair.

After nine months the Ethiopians asked us to return to our village. The Sudanese man had asked me to go to Sudan with him but I refused. I stayed on in Massawa for a while and then I and my children returned to Demas. There I began a business selling tea, *suwa* and food – that is how I managed to live.

Ogba's experience of oppression and her forced identity as a Muslim simply because a Muslim man had raped her, show clearly that she had no identity of her own. She had no right to exist unless she could be categorized as the appendage of a man – a wife or a daughter. Even so, the ultimate determinant of her identity was her sexual "purity", and in the strong religious tension of that period she carried the burden of maintaining the purity of her community. If she was "defiled" it was better that she be disowned by her religious group. But such was the shifting, half-formed structure of this early feudalism that, as her story shows, it crumbled and became irrelevant in the face of war and displacement.

As for the ELF, its bullying tactics and lack of respect for the rural population are recounted by many other women all over the country. For example, Fatma Mohammed Omer from Bagla village in the Rora mountains of Eritrea reminisced about the days when the ELF was the only fighting force:

> At that time of course everyone supported the ELF, but no one liked their behaviour. They would come and ask for food. If they

were offered what they thought was too little, they would ask the villagers to cook more. If it was cooked out of millet, they would ask for wheat. The women would have to go and grind grain for them. They would ask for dates and if they did not have money, they would ask for credit. Sometimes they would ask us to kill goats. Later when the EPLF started agitating in the village the ELF asked the people to arm themselves as a militia and "defend themselves against the EPLF". At first we did nothing, we simply played for time. Then we went over to the side of the EPLF and were armed as militias [see later in this chapter]. The EPLF were very different, they came with their own food, they tried to teach us and help us with our own work . . .

The superior attitude adopted by the ELF reflected its total lack of interest in the crucial question of people's participation, and its blind acceptance of the hierarchical and divisive attitudes of the society which had formed its leaders. This led to an organization whose structure was inherently undemocratic and which was incapable of developing a national programme. In the case of its military strategy, for example, instead of building a national army for liberation and through it fostering national unity, the ELF divided its fighting force along provincial, tribal and religious lines. This deepened the already existing divisions and set up long-lasting hostilities and prejudices (for example, among the Kunamas). The decentralized command units were linked to a Supreme Council which was located outside Eritrea and saw no need for democratic structures or even long-term programmes or policy; policy-making was therefore almost non-existent in the ELF. In keeping with this, and as Ogba Habte and Fatma Omer's narratives illustrate, there was no mechanism through which the ELF could be accountable to the people. The masses were expected to follow traditional leaders without question. As for the ELF's attitude towards women's participation, at first it refused to accept women into the movement, and when they were finally allowed to join, the attitudes they faced made it impossible for them to participate as equals. It was this essentially feudal approach too which led to the ELF's eagerness to kill anyone who disagreed with it –

even potential allies. In 1965 when the ELM sent armed units to participate in the struggle they were wiped out by the ELF; and the persecution of dissidents within the ELF went on right through the 1970s.

Nothing could stop the tide of nationalism which swept through the country, however, and this was eventually indirectly responsible for transforming the struggle. By the late 1960s and early 1970s thousands of young people were leaving their homes, eager to join the movement. Among them were workers and unemployed people from the towns, as well as peasants and students. In terms of social forces, they included people who had been affected by the class struggles of the 1950s and as such had a more progressive outlook than the ELF leaders.

Of the students, a small but significant number were from the University of Addis Ababa. The contribution of this group (who joined the ELF in the late 1960s and the EPLF after it was formed in 1970) was important. They had been deeply involved in the unique student politics at the university; unique because Ethiopia was a monarchy with no political parties, so the students' union played a special role in mobilization and politicization. Also, from the mid-1960s onwards the country was edging towards revolution (a revolution which was to remain incomplete, pre-empted by the military coup of the Dergue). In this situation the subject of self-determination for Eritrea had become a crucial issue of debate. Among the EPLF cadres who belonged to this particular group of students was Petros Georgis. Addis in those days, he told me,

> was very much a neo-colonial town. Apart from the imperial buildings, it was like a collection of villages linked by new roads. There was massive foreign investment in Ethiopia at the time so there were a number of new buildings but behind the buildings there were a lot of huts. The Americans were setting up the armed forces, the police were being trained by the Germans, the air force by the Americans and Swedes. The Western Allies were building Ethiopia in their own image – the worst aspects of their own image.

Since 1953, when Haile Selassie had agreed to provide America with a military base, the United States had started pouring military and economic aid into Ethiopia. By the mid 1960s the Ethiopian armed forces were among the largest in Africa. US private investment had moved in. US government agencies had established themselves and were able to influence not only the state but many sections of society. In other words, the United States had gained almost total control over Ethiopia, and the Kagnew military base in Asmara was wholly outside Ethiopian jurisdiction.

At the same time, Ethiopia (unlike Eritrea) had a social formation characteristic of full-fledged feudalism, with an established feudal class and feudal institutions. These were now drawn into a typically neocolonial framework through the growth of a vast centralized bureaucracy. As Markakis and Ayele write,[14] this had a conventional form with various government institutions but:

> to manage these institutions a class of civil and military officials was required who could fulfil the exacting role of royal retainers, that is to wield great power without possessing it . . . this task was meticulously performed by a group of men especially recruited and groomed for this purpose by Haile Selassie himself.

A new class which Markakis and Ayele call the "military-bureaucratic bourgeoisie" grew round this inner core of retainers. Contradictions began to grow between them and the bulk of soldiers who were recruited from the peasantry and suffered considerable hardship.

At the same time many feudal institutions continued unchanged. For example the Church still functioned as an apparatus of the state. Church buildings were adorned with pictures of the emperor and each had a role in celebrating the monarchy. Prostitution also continued to flourish, adapted and expanded to meet the needs of the neocolonial ruling elites. Haile Selassie's foreign minister is said to have been given the task of finding prostitutes for foreign dignitaries – particularly during conferences of the Organization of African Unity.

In the middle of all this was the University of Addis Ababa. As Petros Georgis told me:

It was a place for students seeking status. Even if a student was poor he could expect to become a part of the establishment after going through university. We had to wear a suit (for most students probably for the first time in their lives), a blue suit with the badge of the University of Addis Ababa.

University students represented a particular section of the petit bourgeoisie: they were mainly of urban origin and a product of the post-war period. As Petros described, they enjoyed unrestricted and automatic access to public employment. The starting salary of a university graduate, regardless of professional specialization or branch of service, was 500 Ethiopian dollars per month. At that time the per-capita income was only 150 Ethiopian dollars per annum.[14] However, by the late 1960s Ethiopia's cash-crop economy began to feel the effects of the trade depression which followed the closure of the Suez Canal in 1967. As a result the civil service and state enterprises could no longer be expanded and since they were already virtually saturated with graduates, students leaving Addis Ababa University no longer had well-paid jobs waiting for them.

While this was one cause of the radicalization of the student community, another, as Petros puts it, was:

> a certain element of consciousness being transferred to the university from Eritrea. You can imagine in 1966 demonstrations for land reform were taking place in Addis and the first few lines of the demonstration, those who would bear the brunt of any attack, were all Eritreans. In a way the university experience also helped Eritreans studying there to articulate their political direction – open debate was permitted and there were a large number of progressive students from other African countries who had come on scholarships. It must also be remembered that when the trade unions in Eritrea were banned, many leaders of the movement migrated to Addis and helped set up trade unions there. . . . There was popular support for the ELF but at first there was very little information about it because ELF activities were outside the popular struggle which was in the cities. Then their line became clearer and students

– just a few – started joining in 1966-7. Then we started getting messages about problems within the ELF. Our strategy at that time was to support the armed struggle but at the same time join hands with the Ethiopian progressives to overthrow Haile Selassie, to democratize Ethiopian society, so we could legitimately ask for self-determination. "Land to the tiller" was chosen as a rallying slogan. As I said, some of the best progressives from all over Africa were there, and they became the driving force radicalizing the Ethiopian students.

Worku Zerai, later one of the first women in the EPLF, was deeply involved in the student movement. But as she explained:

The participation of women was on the whole very low. I think this was because the Ethiopian struggle was not a colonial question but a class issue, and women are often lacking in such struggles.[15] In fact even on Eritrea, the Ethiopian students took a long time to recognize it as a colonial question. In the sixties most of them saw it as one of many nationalities within Ethiopia. But by the early seventies the student movement had [started to] recognize colonialism in Eritrea. This was one of the main reasons, although there were others, for the massacres of students in Ethiopia in the mid-seventies.

In the late sixties the state's attitude to women activists had also changed. . . . In Asmara, women had participated all through, side by side with men, in strikes, sit-ins and so on, but in the fifties soldiers were not arresting women. The women would refuse to part from their male comrades and sometimes when they were arrested and their parents came to see them, the police would ask them to go and they would refuse to leave. But in the second half of the sixties opposition to the state was stronger, repression was harsher, and Haile Selassie started attacking women too. This was the turning point; after this, men and women were treated the same.

With the students' movement gathering strength and a City Wide Union set up uniting all students, the aim of fighting for the rights of people all over Ethiopia was officially established. Petros Georgis said:

Until 1967 Eritrean students were at the forefront of this, but after that the Ethiopian security got very active – they were trying to appeal to Ethiopian students by saying that they were being used by Eritrean secessionists. Then Eritreans decided at a secret meeting to support the students' union but not to be at the forefront or in the leadership. The right to self-determination continued to be discussed but by Ethiopian students. An Ethiopian student leader called Waliling discussed it openly in front of 2,000 students. It was too much for the state. He and seven others were arrested and after that the union was constantly closed down and reopened. It had become a threat to the emperor. Now it was not only university students but also school students who were politicized . . . but unfortunately it was only a students' movement, not a party. There was no political party in Ethiopia and as a students' movement it had reached its climax.

In 1969–70, when the students' movement was at its height and the state faced a major economic crisis, the situation demanded a revolutionary party to launch armed struggle. But no such party existed. Instead, students, workers and other progressive elements came together as a loose-knit popular movement. The crisis deepened, and a terrible famine began in rural areas. The reasons for this were not only the failure of the rains and the backward social formations which divided cultivable land into smaller and smaller plots, but also the appropriation of land from the peasants and pastoralists for cotton plantations run by foreign companies. In autumn 1972 a report prepared by the Ministry of Agriculture and the United Nations' Food and Agriculture Organization warned of impending famine and calculated the amount of grain required to prevent it. The government suppressed the report, however, and grain held in storage was not sent out to the affected areas. In 1973 starving peasants began to arrive in the capital, only to be turned away by the government. At this time an underground party which was to become the Ethiopian People's Revolutionary Party (EPRP) was at last beginning to be formed. It was too late, however: within a year the Dergue, a military committee, was to come to power on the back of the popular movement, cloaked in its rhetoric.[16]

The Dergue excluded and eventually destroyed the working class and student movements. It comprised people from a lower feudal background than the earlier government, and also drew in a large number of lumpen elements at various levels of the state, co-opting a few radical intellectuals who enhanced its progressive rhetoric. However, its ideology was in fact a populism which was inherently right-wing. These fascist tendencies were to become dominant as the years passed.

The United States decided to support the new government, but with changes in the region the Dergue was to swap camps and by 1978 it was receiving massive Soviet aid. Economically Ethiopia has continued until now with its old cash-crop economy and has remained in that sense a typical neocolony of the West. Officially, however, it is a "communist" country, though this does not mean transformations from below. The reforms talked about in early years have been either abandoned or neutralized, with a growing concentration of power in the hands of the Dergue. The mode of production has remained typical of a semi-feudal neocolony. "Communism" turned out to be merely a fanfare, with the hammer and sickle, and Red Squares in every town and village; and fanfares are a part of feudal ideologies.

Not surprisingly, in terms of Eritrea the Dergue continued the same policy as Haile Selassie, displaying the same brutality, paranoia and chauvinism. In the midst of these dramatic changes the EPRP continued to organize for armed struggle. On the Eritrean question it was still somewhat uncertain. As Worku told me: "they finally decided to ask Eritreans to work separately".

By this time Worku was involved with the EPLF; she had joined in 1971.

> Some Eritreans leaving for the field had approached me and I had joined. . . . They made arrangements for me to work with the EPLF representative in Addis. So I had continued my work with the students' movement and started also doing clandestine work for the EPLF – distributing pamphlets, finding out information, recruiting

fighters and so on. I recruited two vice lieutenants in the Ethiopian army. Some people had told me that they were interested so I approached them. It was dangerous. One of them had left behind my first letter to them which had my name and code name. I had told them to burn all their letters, but they had burned the others and left this. A member of one of their families, who did not know where they had gone, searched his bag and found the letter. They came to me and told me to take care. But the Ethiopian security had got to know and people started asking me to leave, even Ethiopians. In March 1973 I finally left Addis.

In early 1975 the EPRP formed its armed wing. According to Petros Georgis:

> The students who formed it went to Sahel [in Eritrea] to get training. They hijacked a plane and went to Sudan, Libya and then Sahel. Six months later, the student leader Waliling and six others including an EPLF cadre from the field tried to hijack another plane. But they were caught and murdered on board by plain-clothes security men.

Among these hijackers were two women. One of them, Martha Mebrahtu, is one of the heroic martyrs of the Eritrean struggle.

With both movements growing in size, the strength and cohesion of the EPLF increased while the divisions within the ELF continued to deepen. Civil war between the two movements raged from 1972 to 1974 despite the massive onslaughts of the Ethiopians. Finally in 1975 the EPLF emerged as the dominant movement. It then began the crucial work of conscientizing and involving the masses. Ande Michael Kahsai, a member of the EPLF Central Committee and then a cadre with the Department of Mass Administration, described to me the new programmes which the EPLF was now able to undertake.

> The Department of Mass Administration, whose task was to organize Eritreans on the basis of their social origin, sent out armed propaganda units into the rural areas. They were responsible for holding public meetings, giving political education and setting up cells. Once they had established themselves in a locality they gradually started implementing their political programme, setting up village assemblies, initiating land reform etc. It was a slow

process. Our unit was responsible for the triangular area of Adi Ugri, Segeneiti and south of Asmara. We held public seminars to acquaint people with what the EPLF was. We found in that period people were not familiar about the differences between the ELF and EPLF. The civil war came to an end around that time. People were emotional; their view was often: "why should you fight each other?" In 1974 about 30,000 people from Asmara and surrounding villages defied the Ethiopian army and went to meet the ELF in the village of Gwoki and the EPLF in nearby Zagar. They urged the two fronts to stop the civil war and join hands against the enemy if they wanted to serve the people. . . . So the focus of our talks had to be the history of the armed struggle, the differences which led to the creation of the EPLF, the differences in political line between the ELF and EPLF.

Gradually we started setting up cells. What people wanted to know at that time was why we needed two organizations. So we had to give them an explanation of the historical development of the ELF, the contradictions within the ELF, the lack of democracy and the persecutions that occurred in the 1960s. And since most of this area had experienced the ELF it was not too difficult. People judge others through their practical actions. They could easily see the difference between the way the ELF cadres treated each other and the equality we had in our unit or the solidarity we had for each other. They commented on this.

That was the first time we went to the South Adi Ugri area. The people there had never seen an EPLF fighter before, nor had any information. There were six of us only. It was an ELF area. We went and had a series of meetings in about twenty villages. In the meetings people would ask us questions. Then when the meeting was over they would take each one of us individually and ask a series of questions. They could see that we had a common outlook. That was one thing which impressed them very much. But even very minor things like sharing a cigarette meant a lot to them. Because with the ELF they had seen that anybody with money could buy anything. The EPLF units would hold meetings and then we would go – leave the area. Their interpretation was that we cared about the security of the people and our own security, whereas the ELF troops would spend the night in a place where the Ethiopian troops were close by. Also we had our own supply of food – we did not depend on the people. And they also noticed that our approach was one of persuasion. People would come, especially the youngsters, with a million questions. And the EPLF fighters would be willing to answer them.

At that time there were no women in our unit, in fact there were hardly any women in the whole EPLF. Recruitment of women was very difficult in the countryside. Even now there is a barrier to women's participation – at that time political affairs were seen entirely as a male domain.

The cells set up by the armed propaganda units were to evolve into the mass organizations, the national unions, which are now not only extremely strong and well-organized but are autonomous from the Department of Mass Administration. The National Union of Eritrean Women (NUEW) is responsible for the political representation of women on a national and regional level (see Appendix 5). The embryonic unions – the cells – were the first step towards establishing what the EPLF calls "People's political power". This concept of people's political power is seen as being central to the transformation of the woman's position, to the release of the creative energy of the masses, and in fact to all social, political and economic change. It is implemented through the people's assemblies which, as we shall see, are responsible for all political and adminstrative decisions pertaining to civilian life.

The EPLF was not operating in a vacuum. Eritrean villages already had an adminstrative structure, laid down initially by the Italians and later modified by the Ethiopians, and in some areas even by the ELF. The ramifications of this administrative structure are interesting but not essential, if one is seeking to understand the changes which were undertaken. It is enough to single out the official at the bottom of the administrative ladder and look at his role. He was the *chika* or *dagna*, and belonged to one of the powerful indigenous clans. He was appointed on the death of his father and when he died he was replaced by his son, or if he had no son then by the son of a close relative. He was a judge, arbitrating on all land disputes, divorces and quarrels on the basis of customary law. He charged each party, a dollar in addition to bribes in most cases and sometimes levied substantial fines. He was also an administrator who collected government taxes. Since he kept a tenth for himself as his salary, his interests and those of the higher authorities overlapped. He was definitely a representative of feudal and colonial power.

It was in villages with this type of administrative set-up that the EPLF established its first cells. The cells then began the gradual process of politicizing the masses and mobilizing them in terms of class and group. In areas involved in settled agriculture for example, the EPLF distinguished four main classes: feudal landlord, rich peasant, middle peasant and poor peasant. Poor peasants, about 60% of the population, were those who had very few possessions, owning at best one ox and a small plot of land. Middle peasants owned 2 to 4 oxen and about 5 acres, and rich peasants owned more than 4 oxen and more than 5 acres of land.

At the same time intense education campaigns were launched, explaining the function and role of the assembly which was to be set up. All this took time and it was not before 1977 that the first people's assemblies actually appeared on the scene.[17] Their composition depended on the relative size of each class and group in the village. It was therefore inevitably tilted in favour of women and poor peasants, because the number of poor peasants and women was inevitably much larger than the number of rich and powerful men in the village. To quote an example from an EPLF document: "If the poor peasants number 60, the middle peasants 30 and the rich peasants 10 the People's Assembly would include 6 poor peasants, 3 middle peasants and one rich peasant."[18] While the peasant delegates can include women, women are also separately represented on the people's assembly as delegates of the NUEW, again categorized as rich, middle and poor. (Before 1987 women could hold dual membership of the NUEW and any other union, but this is currently not permitted.)

The establishment of a people's assembly was described to me by Askalou Woldu from Degsana village near Beleza as part of her life story:

I can't say I knew anything about Eritrea or Ethiopia before 1975. Or perhaps I should say that I never thought of participating. I was conscious of the killings of students and of Eritreans in general. I remember all the demonstrations and protests but I did not participate.

I had been engaged before I was born, and had an arranged marriage with no consultation but there was love between us . . . In 1975, one morning after breakfast my husband went to work, never to return. He was imprisoned and I did not know his whereabouts. I had five children and although his family helped me, I could not live alone.

I went to live with his family in the countryside, in Degsana village. At that time, in 1975, the fighters were coming and going. Soon after I went there I got involved with the Women's association. Women from the Department of Public Administration used to come. They would sit with us and talk and explain about colonialism and about women's oppression. They would hold meetings and discuss with women and men.

After the Women's Association was formed we started organizing all the women. We had education for all women about our position in society, about our role in the revolution and also about what our future life could be.

By late 1976 or early 1977 the People's Assembly was set up. I was a member of the executive committee. Before the election the men's attitude was that women could not be equal to men, and women could not represent other women. But after a lot of political education and mobilization, done mainly by the Department of Public Administration, people began to change. Of course [some], particularly the rich men of the village, still resisted, but none the less it was possible to implement the changes. The People's Assembly was composed of the Peasant Association, the Youth Association and the Women's Association. Out of 37 people in the Assembly, 17 were women. There were 12 executive committee members, including the chairperson, vice chairperson and treasurer; of the remaining 9, 3 were judges, 3 were in charge of economic issues – agriculture, the people's shop and so on, 1 was in charge of forestry, 1 of security of the village and 1 of education and social affairs (later education and social affairs were separated).

After the People's Assembly was established, the Women's Association became even more active. We started taking part in the war, looking after the fighters – there were some important strategic places nearby, like Beleza which was a sort of front line. We were also given some land which we worked on together. The income from the harvest on the women's land was given to those who could not support themselves; the remaining money was put into setting up a Women's Association tea shop.

Once set up, how did the people's assemblies actually function? According to the EPLF their aim has been to "organise and direct in practice the radical social changes awaiting materialisation".[18] Perhaps it is this radical change which is reflected in the enthusiasm and excitement with which rural women describe their assemblies and their role within them. Not so long ago, women could rarely expect a hearing from village adminstrations, let alone imagine being adminstrators and arbitrators themselves. As Fatma Omer told me:

Adjudication was never considered women's work, and now it is. I became involved with the People's Assembly in 1980 and was elected. The people wanted me so I accepted. I am responsible for justice on the executive committee of the People's Assembly. There are 13 members of this executive, [and] 2 are women. This is for the Bagla area. On the District People's Assembly there are 5 women. I am a member of both village and district justice committees and also a member of the central committee of the National Union of Eritrean Women. Recently, for example, I adjudicated in the case of a dispute between two men, Adana Fasel and Mohamed Said, over a plot of land. Three of us on the justice committee of the People's Assembly went to see the plot. We then saw witnesses, asked older people who knew the land, and came to the conclusion that it belonged to Mohamed Said.

How is the issue of women's oppression dealt with? Lemlem Hailu from Fishae Merarra village, Semanwi Bahri district, north-east of the Asmara–Massawa road, is on her people's assembly and is in charge of the property of the assembly. She allocates land to those who want to build houses, for example,

Laying the Foundations 53

and food to those who want to hold a feast. She told me of an interesting judicial case which had been brought to the assembly and how they dealt with it:

> There was a family with two children where the woman stopped having children. Her husband started going with other women and having children by them. She told him to stop doing this and to bring these other children and she would look after them. But he did not listen and had one more child. The woman presented the case to the People's Assembly. The People's Assembly asked him to stop behaving like that or else half his property would be given to his wife. He refused. Finally they took over the land, they gave her half the coffee garden and area for producing grain and told her she could do what she liked with it. She sold the coffee garden and gave the rest of the land to be ploughed by others. The rest of the property was also shared. Then she went to her other village (the people of Semanwi Bahri have houses in the highlands and also lower down) and settled there and married again.

There are countless other stories, cases dealt with and lives transformed by a new system of justice. Here I will include only one, a brief account of Teberh Germatsion's experiences:

> I am 43. I was born and brought up in Asmara. My father was a policeman, my mother a housewife. I have had seven children, of whom two died. I went to school up to fourth grade and then my marriage was arranged to my teacher. I was 13 and did not know what marriage was so I was neither for it nor against it. I stayed with my husband for a honeymoon, then went back to my mother for a month and then went back to my husband to start my married life. My husband was 15 years older than me; he used to get drunk and beat me. I ran away to my parents 15 times! Each time they sent me back. After 1975 life in Asmara became very difficult. The situation was bad anyway – to add to it, my husband spent most of his money on drink. I decided to leave my husband and go and live with his parents in their village with my children. In the village my brothers-in-law were tilling the land. They would give me some of their harvest and I would go to Asmara at the end of the month when my husband got his salary and he would give me some of it. But the

money was not enough and trips to Asmara were too risky (see Chapter 4) so I stopped going and we started living on the grain from my brothers-in-law and some money from my parents. Meanwhile I had started working with the EPLF and they also were helping me.

My husband kept asking me to come back but I always refused. After three years my brothers-in-law refused to help me, saying that it was no longer their duty since I had left their brother. I told them to give me the land and I would take care of it. They said: "This land does not belong to you, it is our brother's and you have refused to go back to him." I asked neighbours and friends to help but it was no use. Finally I presented the case to the People's Assembly. Some of his relatives were in the People's Assembly and they came to try and settle the case out of court. But the brothers-in-law refused, so it went to court. I got my husband's land – all of it – on the grounds that I had the children, I got no money from him and we had nothing to eat.

This was in 1980. I started to plough the land (it was three tsimdis) with co-operative help. [One tsimdi is the area a pair of oxen can plough in a day.] I organized my life and then at the end of 1980, my husband came and demanded the children. I refused, [and] fearing the People's Assembly, he left. In 1981 he came again to take them. I reported it to the People's Assembly, of which I was by then a member. I told them: "I don't want to give the children to him because he is a drunkard and also because no one will take care of them. Also, the children wishes must be considered; they should come to the People's Assembly and say what they want." So everyone was taken to the People's Assembly. The children said: "If our mother wants she can go with him, we won't." After that he did not come back.

Two of my eldest children joined the fighting force; the rest were with me till 1982 when I sent them to the Zero School. Then I was alone. I gave my land to the EPLF and started working with them full-time. I am an armed civilian, trained as a member of the People's Militia. I have my own pistol. I have been elected on the People's Assembly three times, twice on the Village Assembly and once on the District Assembly. Later, after the National Union of Eritrean Women became independent from the village administration, I started working full-time with the union.

Teberh's story illustrates so many of the processes of the revolution: the support given by the EPLF to women who rebel; the effect of basic democratic procedures in raising people's consciousness and hopes; and the immense dedication of women like her who have sacrificed everything for the revolution – she in the end had no property, no separate aim of her own – and identified totally with the struggle of the people. Her story also shows us how women's emancipation is intrinsically related to all other aspects of the revolution, from political participation to self-defence.

Teberh joined the people's militia probably around 1980. But let us go back a few years to the period in the mid-1970s when the first people's militias were set up. Apart from their military function, they too must be seen as part of the EPLF's effort to create and enhance people's participation and democracy. Their role has been described by the EPLF as "to provide an armed people's force to guard and defend the village or district [a force which is also] directly involved in production and [to provide] an example of mutual aid and cooperative work"[18].

The establishment of people's militias was an extremely difficult task, not only because it challenged attitudes to women and other oppressed groups and hence required the dismantling of traditional power relations, but because all this had to be done in a countryside riddled with clan-based militia. It demonstrated one of the main differences between the ELF and the EPLF, that while the former simply depended on the support of the traditional village power structure, the latter established a mass base among the people. For example, the most important of the existing militia when the EPLF came into the picture was the Nech Lebash, a militia clothed in white and set up by the Ethiopians. Members of the Nech Lebash lived in their villages and were responsible for keeping their areas clear of guerrillas. If a member of the force died his clan would be responsible for replacing him, in this way using and reinforcing intra- and inter-clan power relations. In the wake of the civil war, as an EPLF document states, the movement was able to:

dismantle the Nech Lebash as an institution of the enemy . . . [by] disarming those members of the defunct Nech Lebash whose outlook and age would not make them fit to accomplish the tasks of the revolutionary people's militia and [reorganised] the remaining majority making the greatest effort to remould them through intensive political education. They were integrated with and put under the leadership of the newly organised and more politically conscious and reliable militia members and thus transformed from instruments of the enemy to important organs of the revolution. In this way the EPLF was able to build a strong, disciplined and [politically] conscious revolutionary armed people's force, in which women participated with equality . . . and enabled the Eritrean masses to see in practice the fundamental difference between the real people's militia and the reactionary militias set up by the Ethiopians and the ELF.[18]

How was the EPLF able to perform this astonishing task? Perhaps ultimately it was because, as the same document comments in passing, "the events of 1974 in Ethiopia and Eritrea had indeed created the most favourable revolutionary conditions in both Ethiopia and Eritrea". Also, with the hegemony of the EPLF and its creation of cells in the rural population, it had become the type of revolutionary party Gramsci had visualized, which had convinced the people to the point when:

> The entire "logical" argument now appears as nothing other than auto-reflection on part of the people – an inner reasoning worked out in the popular consciousness, whose conclusion is a cry of passionate urgency. The passion, from discussion of itself, becomes once again "emotion", fever, fanatical desire for action.[19]

This first process of convincing the people was full of obstacles and difficulties, however. For example, over the issue of women's participation:

a) Since in Eritrean feudal society, women have strong cultural, religious and family pressures – not to leave their homes and not to participate in production, let alone be armed – it can be said that the arming of women was carried out under the hardest of conditions, especially at the beginning. There was widespread talk opposing us, comments such as "our daughters are Sharia (the Koranic Law) women, and their religion does not allow them to go out of the house or go around with men", "they want to make our girls prostitutes, otherwise what enemy can these girls kill? And which man is going to marry them tomorrow?" Some of the first women who took up arms as militia were evicted from their houses by the men and the others were threatened with divorce. All this tremendously slowed down the arming of women.

b) Since the method of arming followed by the EPLF was fundamentally different from the clan based Nech Lebash system of arming which existed with the clan and "maibet" conflicts, some temporary problems were created when reorganising the old Nech Lebash or arming new militias. "So and so's clan has not been disarmed", "this clan has been given areas", "Why should our leaders be from that clan" etc. such grumblings were constantly heard.

c) Long standing land-based conflicts existed, inside and between many villages, tribes and nationalities. The holding of arms indeed aggravated the conflicts. But if the revolution was to arm one side, before the land-based conflict was settled, the result generally was catastrophic. The other side endeavours to arm itself at any cost.[18]

With the tensions between the ELF and EPLF continuing although now on a lower ebb, the information essential to distinguish between the two movements was unfortunately still very scarce even in the mid-1970s. Often people joined the movement most accessible to them geographically. What were their experiences if this movement happened to be the ELF and how did they see the civil war between the ELF and EPLF? And what specifically were the experiences of women within the ELF? Ghdy, now an EPLF cadre but once an ELF combatant told me her story.

My family are from the middle level of peasants in Amfona in the province south of Asmara. We had a pair of oxen, 40 sheep and some land. We were always conscious of Ethiopian oppression. There was an army camp near our village and we had to face constant humiliation. In the extended family the women's work was very hard and exhausting. Rearing the children, working in the fields clearing, cutting, and carrying water sometimes from very long distances. After the day's work the woman would have to come home and cook. My mother would warm the water and wash my father's feet. Most girls would be engaged before they were 9 and married before they were 15. They had no right to say anything. basically money was the issue – a dowry had to be paid to the husband's family – if it was too low, the girl's life would be made a misery. She could be beaten and insulted and told: "you came empty-handed".

I went to a school, first in a village close by. About a third of the children were girls but gradually they began to stop coming as they got engaged and then married. Later I went to school in a bigger village to continue my education up to eighth grade. I lived in a hostel. And then [I went] to a small town, Decemhare, for secondary schooling. By this time there was only one girl for every eight or ten boys. It was in secondary school that I started getting politically conscious. It was a time when the armed struggle had started. In fact it was 1970, the year which saw the birth of the EPLF. It was also a time of some of the most brutal reprisals by the Ethiopians.

In Decemhare there was a big army camp. When the soldiers got drunk they would be violent – there was constant conflict between students and soldiers. In 1973 many students joined the EPLF. But really it was very difficult to differentiate between the EPLF and ELF; we received pamphlets from both and joined whichever one happened to be nearer.

[In 1972, with all these tensions around her, Gdhy failed her matriculation.] I left Decemhare and went to Addis for work. I got a job teaching in a private school. I taught for two years. In this phase the oppression was more visible and I felt it more because I had become acutely politically conscious – I felt I was a foreigner in Addis. In 1975 after the overthrow of Haile Selassie I joined the ELF. With the nationalistic urge and the desire to fight pushing me forwards, I did not choose between the ELF and EPLF. I simply wanted an opportunity to express my feelings. I took a bus to Adigrat in Tigray, 190 km from Addis, and then went on foot to the border. When I crossed the border the ELF met me. I was registered and taken to the rear areas; there I found many other women also waiting to join. Eventually we were told that because the number who wanted to join was too high, we would not be allowed to join. But we insisted, we really insisted and in the end, 60 women were taken to a training camp southwest of Asmara in Serai province. Thousands of young people were joining so there was only one month of military training. Between January and April 1975, 7,000 joined the ELF alone. (The EPLF was small at that time.) When I joined, about 300 girls were receiving training; the oldest were about 23. After our training was over I was assigned to the security department in the highlands around Asmara. My job was identifying spies because the enemy was also sending students to join the ELF.

Since there was no political training, the attitude of men to women was unchanged; it was exactly as it was in society in general. On the one hand we were assigned with the men to carry guns but on the other hand it was very difficult to work if you were a woman. For example, when you gave your report it would not carry the same weight as that from a man.

Again, although sexual contact was forbidden on pain of death because of poor discipline, there were cases of sexual harrassment. Because there was no political education we also had no base for the future. Most leaders were intellectuals – they did not know the peasant cadres, they did not understand the problems of the masses and the people did not understand them. After about a year, however, they decided to start some political education. I was transferred to the political department, given some very quick political training, and asked to go round teaching politics in the training camps. This was something new for the ELF at that point. This was when they also started mass organizations linked to the ELF.[20] They created an organisation of women – fighters and women from the mass organizations. It was called the Eritrean Womens Association. So women who were fighters were now represented simply as women, not as fighters. did not agree with the idea of such an organization, nor did other women, first because it was ineffective and inefficient, and second because I felt that women fighters did not need to be under such an organization since they were already under the discipline of the army. In theory this organization was fighting women's oppression but in practice it was a tool in the hands of the reactionary leadership. In any case I never joined this organisation, and I was not alone. There were many women who did not accept it although the leadership tried to force it upon us.

All this was happening between 1976 and 1977. At this time there was also a lot of conflict within the ELF over other issues, particularly that of unity with the EPLF. A large section of us ordinary fighters wanted unity but a reactionary leadership refused. In 1977 there was a military battle in Senhit – the leadership and their faction encircled us and started attacking us. I was wounded with bullets in both legs. Comrades carried me for five hours, carrying their guns and me! They took me to the EPLF. I was treated in the Central Hospital in Saloma in Senhit. It took eight months to cure me. I was then given political education by the EPLF for three months. There I learnt the true political history of the EPLF because previously in the ELF we had been taught only to hate the EPLF. We were taught political principles which we had not learnt before.

I was still not able to walk so I was assigned to the revolutionary school to teach. At that time there was the strategic retreat so I was then sent to the Social Affairs Department. There, with 1,000 fighters we sat learning politics, studying and teaching each other. I stayed there almost one and a half years until 1980; then the wounds were cured. I was given three months' training and then sent to the central hospital in the south as a barefoot doctor. I was sent in a mobile team to the front line to care for the wounded. This was in the base area, six or seven kilometres from the fighting where sometimes the big guns reached us. Then I came here to the pharmacy in Orota.

Do I hear from my parents? I left my parents; I never see them. For me they are not different from the people of Eritrea. Of course as parents they were sad not to see me. My village is now in a liberated area. In 1975 it was almost liberated but during the strategic retreat the Ethiopian army could come in sometimes. But not after 1976.

My husband works in the economic sector about 70 km away. He was wounded during the battle of Massawa, and we were together in the National School. During the sixth offensive of the enemy we decided to get married. . . . Every year we have a month together. Our comrades prepare our food and give us a place to live and we live like husband and wife – it is a honeymoon, at his place or at my place. We have had this holiday four times – twice at his place and twice at mine.

In the EPLF people are trained in basic political consciousness. Comrades support and love each other. Women are free to do what they like. They can fight; they can work; they can share the opportunities which the organization provides equally with the men and they can lead. In the EPLF women lead units. They are not shy; they have broken the chains.

4 Behind the Enemy Lines

Writing of the building up of anti-colonial struggle, Fanon in 1961 described the interaction of city and countryside.[21] First there is the formation of an underground party offshoot of the legal (bourgeois nationalist) party. Then its members move away from the cities to escape the police,

> towards the countryside and the mountains, towards the peasant people . . . a people that is generous, ready to sacrifice themselves completely, an impatient people with a stony pride. . . . The men coming from the towns learn their lessons in the hard school of the people at the same time these men open classes for the people in military and political education . . . but in fact the classes don't last long, for the masses come to know once again the strength of their muscle and push their leaders into prompt action. . . . The armed struggle has begun . . .

> The rebellion which began in the country districts will filter into the towns through that fraction of the peasant population which is blocked on the outer fringes of the urban centres, that fraction which has not yet found a bone to gnaw in the colonial system. It is within this mass of humanity, this people of the shanty towns at the core of the lumpen proletariat that the rebellion will found its urban spearhead. For the lumpen proletariat, that horde of starving men uprooted from their tribe and their clan, constitutes one of the most spontaneous and one of the most radically revolutionary forces of a colonised people. So the pimps and hooligans, the unemployed and the petty criminals, urged on from behind, throw themselves into the struggle for liberation like stout working men. These

workless, less-than-men are rehabilitated in their own eyes and the eyes of history. The prostitutes too and the maids who are paid two pounds a month, all the hopeless dregs of humanity, all who turn in circles between suicide and madness will recover their balance and march proudly in the great procession of the awakened nation.

Fanon's model, based on the Algerian revolution, has become famous all over the world. But the reality of the Eritrean struggle stands in stark contrast to it, however one may choose to interpret or adapt it.

First, from the very beginning there were major differences in the concrete conditions in the two colonies. Algeria was a settler colony where the brutal and blatant racism of the French had given rise in every part of society to an overwhelming hatred of and anger against the colonizers. Eritrea had been for years an Italian settler colony, but it was never a settler colony of Ethiopia. Second, while there were definitely no-go areas in Algeria, such as the Casbah in Algiers, the struggle did not last long enough for the development of liberated areas as in Eritrea or in China.

In Fanon's account the first stage of the struggle spread through the countryside like wildfire and then culminated in the immensely important insurrectionary uprising in the city in which the lumpen proletariat played such an crucial role. In Eritrea, apart from the "terrorist" activity of the Group of Seven which in turn grew out of the labour movement and the historic strikes of the 1950s, operations in the cities were undertaken in response to and under direct instructions from the liberated areas in the countryside. In many cases the armed actions were carried out by EPLF fighters from the countryside who had come in at appointed times specifically for this purpose. Such actions went on right through the 1970s, growing in scope and magnitude with the increasing instability of the Ethiopian government. By the mid-1970s, the period when Haile Selassie was overthrown, EPLF urban activities even dismantled and bodily moved small factories from Asmara to the liberated zone, and in one astonishing operation, released all 1500 prisoners at Sembel, the men's prison in Asmara. However, although these actions were crucial, at no time were they central to a struggle which had many equally important and interdependent aspects.

To understand the Eritrean experience in this respect, let us look first at the concrete reality of the cities and specifically at Asmara in the 1970s. What kind of place was this now legendary city? Even a casual reminiscence of Asmara suggests that it was very different from Algiers with its clearly defined urban identity, where as Fanon puts it a fraction of the peasant population was blocked on the outer fringes seeking jobs. Asmara had two parts. The urban European-style city centre which was built and once populated mainly by Italians; and around it, in typical reflection of the uneven development of neocolonialism, a conglomeration of semi-villages, where people had farms and cows wandered undisturbed. The central part of the city incorporated what Petros Georgi's described to me as "a sort of ghetto" but again not populated by a lumpen class:

> Apart from the city centre and the outlying villages, there is also a sort of ghetto area called Abashawel. The people there migrated from the countryside, people who lost their land or women who were divorced and had no means of living. They come and live theré and work as servants or as guards in government institutions. They are more working class than anything else although there is also prostitution and *suwa* is sold. But they bring up their children properly, they are responsible people and there is not that much crime either.

In this kind of city the rural suburbs are not areas where those who work in the cities reside, but are essentially villages which have clustered themselves round other villages. Some of the residents have good jobs in town (bus drivers, government servants, barbers and so on), and thanks to them more ready cash is available. This has not served to change the mode of production, however, but only to intensify the old feudal values: increasing dowries, for example, and intensifying the oppression of women. Asmara typifies the incorporation of feudal values and even feudal relations within the framework of colonial capitalism.

Sara Indrias, who worked in the rural suburb of Mandafera as a social worker between 1976 and 1981, told me what women's lives were like:

> Mandafera was an area of farms, some big farms which employed workers but most of them not very big. The people were middle-class on the whole; many were government servants. The women accepted their lives as women. They were taught from childhood by the Church and by the family to accept that girls are less than boys, women less than men. It was like that in 1976, [and] probably still is even today. Almost all women in Mandafera at that time, even government servants' wives, were illiterate. In 1976 the Ethiopian government started a literacy campaign[22] and part of my job was to teach women to read and write. . . . At that time there were girls who could meet and get to know boys, but 90% had arranged marriages. Dowry was higher in the towns and was dependent on the economic status of the boy. For a highly placed boy there was a big dowry: for example, cows. The boy's family had to give ornaments and the amount of this depended on the economic position of the girl's family. The dowry was often a cause of conflict and many families disagreed and even separated over it. The boy's family looked for a girl whose family had land and were well-off. In Asmara they also wanted an educated girl. Appearance was not that important, but virginity was. There were cases in Mandafera where if the bride did not bleed on the wedding night she could be sent back.
>
> Among the agricultural workers some were women. They did everything except ploughing, but women could never own land. If they separated from their husbands they had to go back to their families and be dependent on them.

In the 1970s this was the position of women, laid down by tradition and implemented by the traditional power structure of the family. Women struggled, and a few challenged this structure but were isolated as individuals. Meanwhile, outside the home the power structures of the Ethiopian state were being shaken. A process had started whose upheavals were to change profoundly the lives of Eritrean women and men, ultimately dismantling both class and family structure. In Asmara, outside the most prosperous enclaves, hunger and unemployment were hitting the people. Essential commodities were in short supply, and production had dropped. It was the expected result of the 20 years when the economy had been looted, first by the British and then by the Ethiopians after the annexation of Eritrea. Factories had been transferred wholesale from Eritrean towns to Ethiopia, and crucial personnel, some of them Eritreans, had been transferred to posts in Ethiopia where the Ethiopians thought they could be kept under surveillance and prevented from supporting the liberation movement.

Although people were suffering in the cities, those living in the countryside were much worse off. The Eritrean Liberation Front (ELF) and EPLF were taking on the Ethiopian army and the regime responded with massive attacks on the civilian population. Villages were being bombed or burnt, and in some areas people were assembled at gunpoint and massacred or asked to leave their villages immediately. Elsewhere, helpless peasant families were pursued for miles by Ethiopian soldiers in tanks and rocket-launchers. All over Eritrea the fleeing, the never-ending travelling, the displacement, the dislocation had begun, and it was to go on for the next 20 years. Class structure, always rather diffuse and changeable, began to have even less meaning. People poured into towns. The lumpen proletariat of cities like Karen and Asmara was now a vast conglomeration of people with different histories and different class and regional backgrounds. Always a class in transition, the lumpen now comprised not only temporary or casual workers, fresh arrivals from outlying rural areas seeking jobs, and permanently unemployed or unemployable city dwellers who might turn to crime. It also included refugees from the war who, unlike refugees from a drought or famine, came with pain, anger and determination to resist. Class hierarchies now became a thing of the past, dissolved by the experience of the war; few would return to the old structures. Although most people still hoped to go back to their home villages when Eritrea became free, often all they had to return to were memories and a location, a particular part of the land with its hills and river and sky; all else was gone. There was also a deeper, more fundamental change: in themselves, in their consciousness, and in their view of the world and the future.

Fifty-year-old Maharite Tekhle and forty-year-old Gaddam Okobalidet, from Ajerbub village north-east of Karen and now in Fil Fil refugee camp, spoke movingly of these changes in their lives.

Mahante: "We are Billens. Our village is two hours' walk from Karen. Under Haile Selassie's regime the Ethiopians were massacring us; they made us gather in churches and mosques and shot us. We had no peace to till our land, and many of us had to flee to Sudan. Under the Mengistu regime many more of our villagers have been killed."

Gaddam: "Because the village is so near Karen everyone even suspected of supporting the Front is arrested. It has been problem after problem. After killing us, torturing us, they say they are doing us a favour. They ask us to sing and dance and ullulate in celebration."

Maharite: "Since the Ethiopians have come we have no peace. They forced us to leave our land, leave our village. Our harvest, cattle and goats have all been taken by the Amharas. Since our peace was disturbed we are always thinking about change. Since we came on the side of the revolution seven years ago, we learnt to be alert, to go out of our houses, to run away . . ."

Gaddam (tears coming to her eyes): "Now there are no Billens in the village. The Amharas are there, the village is destroyed, and even the forest from which we fetched firewood, even the forest is gone. . . . When we get our independence we'll be able to tackle all our problems. We are lucky we are here in Fil Fil" (a refugee camp). "The EPLF looks after us but many are sheltering under trees and by stones with no food to eat and no plans for the future."

These and many other accounts tell of dislocation, loss and longing, and also a formidable strength. This is the story of rural Eritrea. Only personal histories and specific experiences differ, and with them the way women talk about their lives – their openness or reticence, their imagery or incisive analysis, bringing home the richness of the Eritrean experience.

Sembatu Bakheet comes from a very different background. She is 54, a Tigre Protestant and EPLF cadre, a quiet woman of immense dignity who lived in Ghabub, another village near Karen. She told me of the notorious Ona massacre and the simultaneous destruction of her village, and what these atrocities did to her life:

> I was brought up and married in Ghabub village. My father had a shop selling essential commodities like sugar, coffee and oil. My mother was a housewife. There were about ten other shops; the rest of the villagers were farmers and so was my husband . . .
>
> In 1970, the Ethiopians started shooting in the south. My family and I fled towards Karen. When we reached Forto, the gate to Karen, the people of the village of Masadere told us to gather in an Orthodox church. The Ethiopians then entered the church and killed hundreds with guns and bayonets; we ourselves narrowly escaped death. Then we saw that from Forto the Ethiopians had started bombing Ona with heavy artillery and tanks. They had forced people to gather in an Orthodox church there and then they bombed the church. Seven hundred were massacred; Ona was destroyed. . . . School students went there in defiance of the soldiers and buried the dead.
>
> It so happens that this was the time the EPLF was formed. The kind of life Eritreans were facing at that time made me feel that it was the duty of every Eritrean to work to liberate our country. I joined them and worked with them clandestinely for seven years. When the Ethiopians were forced out of Karen in 1977, I began to work openly and then I went back to my village. But I never told my husband and children; my husband was never involved. In 1975 my eldest son joined the armed struggle but he did not know at that

time that I was involved. Later when I started working openly, my second son also joined.

Are women like Sembatu members of the lumpen proletariat – the class which, Fanon warns, if not taken into account by the movement: "will take part in the conflict but this time on the side of the oppressor"? Are they not rather the movement itself? As always in Eritrea, one is struck on the one hand by the unique relationship between the revolutionary party and the people, and on the other by nationalism so powerful and so integral to the psyche that it is inseparable from the personal struggle to survive. How did this nationalism develop? Was it intense suffering which forged the acute sense of identity? As one woman told me: "My country is a part of me – part of my tears, part of my pain, my hope for the future and my children's future." Everywhere in the liberated zone you see disabled fighters. Almost everyone I spoke to had been either attacked, imprisoned or tortured, or had lost someone close to them. Often it was this event which had made them join the EPLF, or at least this event which they would remember when asked why they joined.

In the clinic for severely wounded fighters in Port Sudan I spoke to three young women: Dattabullah aged 25, Meza aged 20 and Zaid aged 24. Dattabullah was recovering and could walk; the others had back injuries which meant that their chances of walking again were very small. They talked to me about why they joined the EPLF, and how they felt about the struggle and about their injuries.

Dattabullah: "I joined the EPLF in 1978. I hate colonialism, really hate it. It bombed my village and killed my two brothers and one sister. . . . After I had my training, I was assigned to Hal hal near Karen. I was never frightened and even when I was wounded I only felt that I had fulfilled my duty. That was in 1982 in the sixth offensive. . . . When we left our homes it was for an independent Eritrea. Till we get it we won't stop. We may have to struggle 24 hours a day on the front line but we don't mind. We may be tired but we just go on. Here I am a doctor. . . .

Zaid: "Before I left Asmara the Dergue arrested me, and when I was arrested the Dergue killed my sister and brother. I was wounded in face-to-face combat in the 'stealth offensive' – the seventh offensive [in 1983]. I had a bullet in my back."

Meza: "I was living just outside the village of Narialat. My grandfather and grandmother were killed in the church while praying. After it happened I could not stay; I left and joined the EPLF. Before I left home I knew there is just killing and just wounding and there is hunger – so I was prepared. I was wounded in the sixth offensive in north Sahel, wounded in the back. I was unconscious. The place of combat was remote. I was injured at 4 p.m. and I was taken on camel-back to Orota hospital, [which] we reached in the morning. Here I am recovering fast. I learn and teach at the same time – I teach grade two Tigrinya and General Science, and I learn grade eight. I also play the organ."

Zaid: "When I was wounded my comrades accepted me warmly. They gave me blood. . . . I was wounded in the morning, [and] I reached the Central Hospital [in Orota] in the evening. Five or six close friends were injured with me. I spent only one month in Orota, then I came here. When I was there I could not get out of bed; now I can go up and down stairs. Now I am a typist and musician. I would be very very happy to go back to the field."

They laughed warmly, happy in anticipation of returning.

The accounts in these women's stories of Ethiopian attacks on helpless villagers and the sight of young children bombed with napalm, and the haunting sadness of once beautiful towns like Nacfa which have been utterly destroyed, make one realize that this is not just any war motivated by colonial oppression: it is genocide. Behind it is a peculiar hatred and vengence characteristic of the semi-feudal neocolonial Ethiopian state. As the years have gone by the situation has escalated with the concentration of power in the hands of one man, Mengistu. His egotism and capacity to annihilate are a product of his country's political position and social formation. Rape and the humiliation of women are an almost expected part of the violence of a colonial army, but here there is an intense, inhuman cruelty which pushes even the perpetrators, the Ethiopian soldiers themselves, to the edge of stability. In Asmara in the 1970s (and in some respects even today), Fanon's specific psychiatric skills in studying the oppressors would have been particularly useful. There the individual Ethiopian soldier "turned in circles between madness and suicide" – often killing themselves after murdering Eritrean women and children.

According to a young woman who had been a member of a clandestine EPLF cell in the 1970s,

> They kill your son and they throw his body outside your house; you are not allowed to cry. . . . The EPLF were doing operations in the city so the Ethiopians attacked the whole Eritrean population – all the people in an area would be rounded up and massacred. There was a curfew. Anyone who went out after curfew would be killed and thrown on the street. On the slightest excuse the soldiers would go on a rampage.

Lemlem told me of one Friday night in 1975 when she was visiting her mother in Asmara: "There were some gunshots from fighters. The Ethiopian soldiers went mad; they went from house to house searching, killing, disembowelling pregnant women. This went on for four days – the streets of Asmara were washed with blood."

Anything could spark off a spate of killings: a fight; an Ethiopian soldier rejected by an Eritrean women; even an intellectual argument in the university.

> There was an argument between students and lecturers about which language was older and more established. An Eritrean lecturer, Dr Petros, said in his lecture [that] Tigre was the oldest, then Tigrinya, then Amharic. The Ethiopian students were angry about this [as] they wanted to be told that Amharic was the oldest. At that time the soldiers on their own initiative constituted themselves into a murder squad: they would kill people

by electrocuting them with a wire round the neck. Dr Petros was the first victim but many other people were also killed. There was terrible tension because no one knew who would be picked up next.

It was in this atmosphere of fear and instability, with social and class structure constantly shifting, with families split up and friends torn apart, and where death and madness lay in wait at every street corner and behind every curfew, that the EPLF organized its crucial "Behind the Enemy Lines" strategy. It was very far removed from Fanon's spontaneous lumpen uprising and was based if anything on an adaptation of the model used in the Vietnamese revolution.

The central unit was the armed propaganda unit. Its role was mobilization, politicization, creation of clandestine cells and co-ordination of armed action. The unit itself was part of a much broader programme of organizing Eritreans according to their social origin, carried out by the Department of Mass Administration. In Chapter 3 we saw how in the early 1970s after the civil war between the ELF and EPLF had broken out and the EPLF had chosen Sahel as its base, cadres of the Department of Mass Administration constituted as armed propaganda units carried out political education, held public meetings and set up cells. (These cells have gradually evolved into the national unions and have become autonomous, so now in the 1980s the role of the Department has changed to one of guidance.)

The methods used to set up cells and the tasks allocated to these cells were very different in the cities from those in areas of the countryside far from the Ethiopian army. In the cities obviously there could be no open recruitment and there was always a danger of Ethiopian infiltration. Cells were often organized around people's jobs: for example, cells of engineers, pharmacists, factory workers, and even managers of companies. There were also cells consisting of women, or of people drawn from a particular locality. Unlike cells in the countryside where participation of women was low, in the cities many more women were able to take part. Their tasks included creating political awareness; collecting information about the enemy; fund-raising; collecting essential items such as medicines for the fighters in the field; and the planning and sometimes execution of guerrilla activities.

Saba Asier, now working in the office of the general military staff, was involved in clandestine work from 1976 onwards. She used to work in her brother's pharmacy as a cover. In 1982 she was arrested and imprisoned for 11 months. Saba described the organizational structure of the cells and some of their work:

> There are five to seven people in a cell. Each person knows only his or her cell members. I became a cell leader and then I became a group leader, dealing with five to seven cells. . . . Above the cells and groups are branches. Each branch has five to seven groups. . . . 1975 – was a time when there were many operations: planting bombs in factories to destroy equipment; putting time bombs in telephone boxes and electricity boxes so that there would be no electricity and no communications; robbing banks and so on.[23]

Right from the beginning, one of the most characteristic aspects of the organization of operations was the close co-operation between the cells and the EPLF fighters in the countryside. Ande Michael, a member of the armed propaganda unit whose job was to set up cells, explained:

> Through the cells we would collect detailed information about the enemy. Some of the cells were armed and if there was an operation sometimes they would carry it out; or more often the cells would conduct the study and commandos from the field would go and carry out the operation. The commando unit was a completely separate unit – they were called the fedayeen.

Since the military strategy of the EPLF focused on participation and protection of the people and conducting protracted war from bases in the countryside, urban guerrilla warfare was never used as a central instrument though it was still essential in specific instances. As Ande Michael commented:

In a situation like ours it is difficult to base yourself on urban guerrilla warfare. This would have led [as it has done in Sri Lanka, for example] inevitably to reprisals and massive numbers of civilian deaths in the towns. At the same time it was important for us to target certain military and economic installations or . . . certain individuals – collaborators with the government, or military officers. And of course there was also fund-raising, recruitment and so on.

Who were the women who became cell members in the 1970s? They came from all backgrounds, drawn in by their harsh experiences and the strength of their feelings. Asmeret Abraham, now a war hero of the EPLF, was among them:

I was born in Asmara and studied there up to the eighth grade. My father was a railway worker in Asmara and my mother a housewife. They are now both dead. Many of my family had already joined the struggle and by the mid-1970s we were facing mass arrests and killings of youths. This situation made me feel a real hatred for the Ethiopians. I preferred to die fighting rather than be killed. But before I could join the armed struggle the EPLF asked me to go back and work in Asmara. I used to distribute leaflets and help supply commodities like sugar to the field. There were Ethiopian soldiers and spies everywhere.

At that time a Tigre man wanted to marry me but I did not want him. He began to give me a hard time, following me around and also spying on me. The EPLF consistently refused to let me join the armed struggle. Then one group of Ethiopian soldiers, the Nech Lebash [white-dressed soldiers] became suspicious of me and started following me. One day when I and two others were taking commodities out of Asmara to the fighters they saw us. They chased us, shooting at us all the time, but we managed to escape and hide in some caves. Luckily we were not wounded. When I escaped the "white-dressed soldiers" I told the EPLF I would never go back to Asmara, first because the soldiers now knew me, and second because of the Tigre man who was harrassing me. After that the fighters kept me with them, though they kept sending me back for various tasks.

The tasks which were part of the urban guerrilla's work were extremely varied. Among the most risky was the recruitment of soldiers from the Ethiopian army, and this was what Asmaret was eventually assigned to do.

> I used to distribute leaflets among Ethiopian soldiers because we were trying to recruit Eritreans who were in the Ethiopian army. Once I was asked to give a letter to an army lieutenant in Shagreni, a small village with several bars, about 19 km from Asmara. I went there and got talking to some of the soldiers. They were Eritrean soldiers in the Ethiopian army, trained by the Israelis as an anti-guerrilla force. They asked me where I was going, and I said: "Asmara". They said: "The way you are dressed you will be in trouble in Asmara." I said: "I was only joking; really I want to meet Lietenant Teklai." They told me: "You won't find him." But I insisted that I must meet him. In the end they took me to a bar and asked me to have a drink. I took a soft drink and sat and waited. He did come to meet me and I gave him a letter, but when he saw the EPLF stamp he was afraid and said he could not read it in front of the others. Where could he meet me later? I told him a place where I would be waiting with two comrades. After some time he came there and met the three of us. He decided to join the EPLF; he brought his gun and a bag of bullets and came away with us.

This remarkable phenomenon, whereby Eritrean soldiers from the Ethiopian army were recruited straight into the EPLF, was characteristic of the mood at the time. It also reflected the EPLF's remarkable success in drawing all potential allies to its side and resolving secondary contradictions; but that is something we shall look at in a later section.

Another task of the cells was fund-raising. Petros Georgis was particularly involved in this because he had a wealthy background and it was thought he would be well able to deal with the rich. He described his work and the incident which led to his being forced to leave Asmara:

> I left Addis and returned to Asmara in 1972. I was working underground. Our cell had seven members. We used to fill our car boots with medical things and pass them on. We would meet

two fedayeen who came armed: Yemane and Memhir Andom. They stayed with us and did their missions while we gave them logistical support. . . . They were two very important fedayeen who came to collect money from a capitalist who owned many buses. He had promised to give 30,000 Ethiopian dollars, but in fact he had told the Ethiopians and they had prepared a trap. So two of my cell members unknowingly drove these two guys to the trap. The businessman said: "I'll bring you some tea", and went out. Then they heard a megaphone announcing that they were surrounded and should give themselves up. They burned their papers and committed suicide . . . they had guns so they shot themselves. The two cell members who were waiting panicked. One of them, Amahatzion, went straight to his house and was arrested. He was tortured to death. The other, Engineer Russom, came straight to my place of work, [and] I drove him to safety in the outskirts of Asmara. I then returned but decided, after consulting my cell members, to leave for the field. Because of my eye problem the decision was made that I should work full-time outside.

Petros was lucky to escape in time. Those who were caught faced the most inhuman torture to try to break them and make them betray their comrades. Nor was there any special consideration for women prisoners; if anything they were treated with greater brutality. These tortures and the conditions prisoners were subjected to were consistently ignored by international humanitarian organizations, other African countries and all agencies who wished to keep on good terms with the Ethiopian government. Saba Asier recounted her experiences in her eleven months of imprisonment:

I was arrested in 1982 on suspicion of being an EPLF member. I was imprisoned in "Mariam Gumbi" – this is a building which used to be a large family house before the Dergue confiscated it from the owners. It is big like a castle and has many underground rooms. There is also a servants' house where the family kept their pigs. The Dergue used the castle for the office and the pig house for the prisoners.

At first they questioned me politely – where I was working, how much money [had] I paid to the organisation, who I was working with, and which pamphlets had I distributed and where? I told them "I know nothing, I just work at the pharmacy. I am not interested in politics. I don't know what you are saying." Then they became angry and took me to the torturing house. For each arrested person there are seven to eight interrogators. They tie your big toes and your hands together, your arms round your legs. Then they put a stick under your knees: this is called the number 8 because your body is in the shape of an eight. They make a ball from the clothes and vomit of prisoners and put it in your mouth. They turn you upside down and then they start beating the bottom of your feet. You hang from the stick which they lay with its ends on two tables. Seven or eight people take turns beating you. When one gets tired, another takes over. On the first night they beat me all night from 5.30 p.m. to 4 o'clock the next morning. They wanted the names of my friends before they could flee from their homes as soon as the curfew was lifted at 6 in the morning. Friends of prisoners flee into the fields until they know whether the prisoner has spoken or not. There are prison workers who are in the clandestine movement. They tell the comrades "the prisoner has spoken" or has not.

The second day at 8.30 in the morning they called me again. They said: "We know that there are others you worked with but you won't tell." They beat me from 8.30 till 12 o'clock. One hour of number 8 and then number 9. In number 9 my big toes were tied together and while I was lying on my belly they stood at the sides of my head and pulled my toes over my back. One man stands on your back. Your hands are tied, they hit your feet with a stick made of leather. As they beat you their hands turn red and sometimes start bleeding. So you can imagine if it hurts them that much, how much it hurts the person that is being tortured.[23]

Tsegat Wind survived a prison sentence of three years. She too had been an urban guerrilla in Asmara.

When fighters came into Asmara I would take them inside the city and help them to hide. I would study the situation for assassination and sabotage, and guide them and follow the operation to the end. . . . In some ways it is worse than fighting in the field because it is inside the enemy. . . . At the end of 1980 I was arrested and sentenced for three years under suspicion. Ethiopian soldiers came to my house at 10 p.m. and surrounded it. My family were there. They took me to prison. At first they began by talking politely and asked if I was a member of the EPLF. They said if I spoke they would release me immediately. When I said nothing they began their torture – torture number 8. They make you sit on the floor with your knees touching your chin and your arms beside your knees. Your toes are tied with rope and your thumbs. They blindfold you. They put a dirty rag with blood and vomit into your mouth to gag you. Then they put a big stick and insert it under your knees and hang you in the air upside down. They begin hitting your soles. Torture number 9. You lie straight on the floor with your hands on your sides. You are gagged and blindfolded. They tie your ankles with a rope and they pull the rope from the front. Then they step on your back and hit your soles. After this torture your soles are swollen and bleeding. They put you down and tell you to walk on the gravel. They tell you to press it hard till the blood starts to spurt out from your soles. In another torture, they tie you up and insert you face-down into a bowl of water. The water is very dirty with blood and vomit. The torturers were men. When you are tortured there is always menstrual flow and it does not stop. They do not give you sanitary towels and there is not enough water to wash . . .

There is also psychological torture. The door is made of iron and it has a chain. When they open it it rattles so every prisoner thinks: "who is going to be called?" because being called means being tortured. After someone is tortured, they bring her and just throw her bleeding and swollen. That in turn affects those inside. Among us there were infants with their mothers, expectant mothers, they too were subjected to the same tortures. There was one woman who was imprisoned with her three-year-old child so whenever his mother went to be interrogated he would cry because they prevented him from going with her and until his mother came back he would cry. Every time they opened the gate he ran to go there, he begged the guards to take him with them and when they didn't he cried.

The interrogation centre Mariam Gumbi is only for political prisoners, men and women. Later the women are sent to Hazhaz prison and the men to Sembel. I spent six months in Mariam Gumbi.

It had three cells and in each cell there were 70 of us. We were allowed to go out to the toilet three times a day and for 15 minutes, but because there were very few toilets often you could not go. In the cell there was a bucket for urinating but it leaked. It used to soil our clothes. We used to be sick with vomiting and diarrhoea. The guards would not provide a new one. It was kept next to the woman who slept closest to the door. In the end we bought one ourselves with money from our parents.

Overcrowding – in Hazhaz there was a space of about 2 feet by 6 feet for each person. If the mattress supplied by our parents was any wider than 2 feet the warders would ask us to cut it. Our parents would also pay the rent of the prison and bring us food, because the food in the prison is very bad. There are people who stay up to a year under interrogation, you can even come back from Hazhaz if they suspect you of anything. My crime was that I was a member of the EPLF, but they also wanted me because they thought I would supply names of other members. I totally denied all charges but they still sentenced me for three years. You don't have a lawyer, they don't take you to court, one day they just come and tell you that you are sentenced.

In Hazhaz there are also prisoners of war. When they are captured at the battlefront they are taken to prison. Those who are wounded are just thrown there; they die or become paralysed or handicapped. In the prison they remove all their clothes and give them a long dress with no sleeves. They have no one outside to buy them clothes or help them. Their parents do not know that they are captured and no one informs them. They themselves do not want to inform them because when they joined the armed struggle they had become socially and economically independent of their families. And since they are not sentenced they do not want their families to support them endlessly. If fighters think the enemy will capture them, they commit suicide. They are the lucky ones. If they are unable to they die like this in prison. In prison it is very difficult to commit suicide. Some go on hunger-strike. Then the guards sometimes come in, take them and kill them. Political prisoners are separated from these prisoners of war.

Can anyone ever fully recover from an experience like this? Tsegat has scars on her arms and feet and a fracture of part of her backbone. After her release in Asmara she had frequent nightmares. If she was at home the sound of a car terrified her, re-creating the scene of her arrest. She left for the liberated zone soon after, where she has been treated. Now she runs the archives of the Mass Administration Department in the liberated zone.

The inhuman violence meted out to women revolutionaries by the supposedly socialist Ethiopian state is far worse than what women activists experienced from the Haile Selassie regime. As the years passed the Ethiopian state has consolidated the culture of a semi-feudal neocolony. The result is a peculiar brutality where society's every-day violence against all women who rebel is extended and intensified in the state's approach to women revolutionaries.

What does rebellion mean in this society? A woman who fights oppression within the family has no outside support, and her rebellion often takes the form of running away. But running away to what? As we have seen in Chapter 3, for a woman wishing to leave her husband and in-laws the alternatives were few and often equally oppressive. Women rebelled through the centuries, but after Italian colonialism all too often this rebellion led nowhere except to the degradation of domestic work and prostitution. Also, rebellion in itself does not necessarily lead to change. As Kate Millet writes in *Sexual Politics*: "To be a rebel is not to be a revolutionary. It is more often but a way of spinning one's wheel deeper in the sand."

From the mid-1970s onwards the existence of the EPLF altered the situation, at least partially. The movement drew many rebel women into the revolution, extricating them from the new exploitations of prostitution and domestic work and so transforming rebellion into revolution.

In relation to the struggle of the Eritrean people the bar-woman was in a unique position. She belonged neither in the world of home and family which were meant to contain all a woman's aspirations and desires, nor in the male world of politics and power. Public life was conducted entirely by men. In villages this meant attending meetings and looking after the communal needs of the area; in cities men went out to work and when their working hours were over they socialized with each other outside their homes.

Elsa, who grew up in Asmara and then in Addis, talked about the separate lives of her father and mother and the subject of male social life in general.

> My father had to work very hard. He would come home for lunch for two hours from 1 O'clock to 3. Then after coffee and a short rest he would go back to work. He finished work at 6 o'clock but he would spend some time with his friends. He came home at 10 or 11 – something like that. I am not quite sure if he was involved with the EPLF because he never spoke about it after he moved to Addis. . . . My mother was very understanding; we were very close to her and we could talk about anything with her. Because my father always came home late we never really talked to him . . . I used to feel very sorry for my mother because she has natural gifts – she is very sensitive and intelligent and strong, but she was always at home cooking and doing the housework. Even though my father had a good job, the housework was very hard, – even lighting the oven with wood or charcoal takes time. Making *injeera* takes hours. The men never do any work at home. Almost all men come home late. If you are depending on them . . . well! My mother couldn't ask my father why he was late or anything. He would be angry because women don't have the right to ask. So we never knew what time he would come. We just had to wait watching TV or something. My mother would wait with his dinner. He might come very late and by that time he might have already eaten.

A woman from Asmara described the following scene to me, a view from her window:

> I lived opposite a bar. The curtain would be only half-way down and my sister and I would watch. Inside were two men, important figures in the Ethiopian government. They had big bellies, they were comfortable in their three-piece suits. The woman of the bar would discreetly usher them into the back room and take

them mead drinks. Eventually they would be joined by a third. They would remain there for hours; then they would leave and we would see them go, pulling their waistcoats over their rounded bellies. We could almost hear them discussing how they were going home to their wives who were busy preparing their meals, keeping the place spick and span and worrying about their being late.

Elsa also told me:

Most children are very close to their mothers, but they can't discuss anything with their fathers. Some men have other relationships, but their wives do not know, they cannot say. Some men have relations with women who work in bars. There are a lot of women who own bars and only women work there – bars are completely different from pubs that way. There is a lot of prostitution in bars. In Addis there are bars on every corner, literally. In Asmara also there are a lot but not so many, and most of them are in the central part of the city – women don't go to bars. People don't respect women they see in bars.

Women were therefore excluded from all informal political life. In this male world of drinking and social and political discussion (which included both Eritrean and Ethiopian men) the only woman present was the bar-woman – there to sell her body, but present nevertheless – the potential guerilla fighter in more senses than one. Where would this potential guerilla fighter have come from, and what experiences and struggles would have placed her in this position and shaped her consciousness? Bar-women were consistently harrassed by the Ethiopian government as suspected supporters of the EPLF. When a woman becomes politically involved she does not leave behind her oppression as a woman. How then did the struggle for liberation of Eritrea interact with the lives of women fighting their oppression as women?

Nebiat is 40. Even if you do not know her you are drawn to her because of her grace and the warmth of her personality. She is one of the heroes of the EPLF. In the 1970s she worked in and later owned a bar in Asmara. In 1987 Nebiat told me the story of her struggles and later when I visited Eritrea in 1989, a close friend of hers from the National Union of Eritrean Women discussed Nebiat's story with me. Nebiat told me:

> I was born and brought up in Asmara and I went to school there till grade six. My father died when I was very young. My parents had not been married and my mother had no job. Eventually she got married to another man. When I was about fourteen my mother arranged my marriage to an Eritrean living in Ethiopia – in fact my husband's stepmother was an Ethiopian. They were a rich family. My mother and my in-laws agreed that they would take me to Ethiopia but not make me sleep with my husband for a few years.
>
> It was all done without my consent and without even my opinion. I was really too young to understand fully what was happening. For one year they kept their promise, then my mother-in-law started telling me to go and sleep with my husband. But I always refused. Then one day my mother-in-law and a friend of hers decided to make me drunk and when I was drunk they gave me to my husband. After that I started sleeping with him. But my life became a life of crying. I felt afraid all the time and I used to cry all the time. I wanted to run away but I had no place to go. If I had I would have run away the very next day. I kept asking them to send me back to my mother. . . . But they wouldn't send me back. My father-in-law was kind to me and so in a way was my husband, but my mother-in-law was jealous, I think, and she started abusing me. Eventually my father-in-law took me back to Asmara to my mother and I refused to return with him. I kept refusing to go back for almost a year and finally they divorced me.
>
> I used to love my mother very very much but after that she started being very harsh to me. She used to make me sleep on the floor and would not let me go out anywhere. But there was a man who used to see me. We were attracted to each other and got involved. He asked my mother for my hand. My mother refused permission. She said: "You have to obey my orders, it is I who knows who is good or bad for you." In the meantime I got pregnant and my mother discovered it. She started to abuse me and beat me and accused me of disgracing the family. She used to make me work very hard, so hard that I got ill. I always had to sleep on the floor. Finally I gave birth to my child but even up to that point her abuses did not stop.

After that she made it impossible for me to stay on in the house. The father of my child rented a small house for me and used to help me with food. Then suddenly, right in the middle of all this trouble I was going through, he got married to another woman. After that I hated to be dependent on him.

I took my child and went from place to place looking for a job office work . . . anything. But it was not possible because you need influence to get a job. Then I decided to start buying drinks like beer and selling them in my house. I started getting to know people. Then the problems started. Men would come and expect me to go to bed with them. I hated it. I had a series of conflicts. I began to feel very frightened and insecure and after some time I decided that it might be safer to work in a bar. The next few years when I was working in the bar, I tried my best to save money. When I had enough I opened my own bar and later a bigger bar. I became totally involved in this work.

From this point in Nebiat's story, her friend intervened from time to time to help me understand the events fully.

Nebiat's friend "Nebiat was still very young and she was so strikingly beautiful. She was much in demand. She told me that she was always careful about her relationships with men. She had long-term relationships with one man, and then if he left, with another. She never slept with many men at one time. Even if she had a date with a new man she never told her long-term one. In this period she started making a lot of money. She bought a car and she started to support her mother and sisters financially. She built her mother a house and her relationship with her improved."

Nebiat: "In this period [1974 to 1976] I started secretly working with the fighters who were entering town – buying commodities for the field and distributing political pamphlets."

Nebiat's friend: "Nebiat was in prison twice. Once when the ELF suspected her of working with EPLF they reported her to the police. She was in prison for a month then, and again later when they suspected all bar-women of hiding bandits."

Nebiat: "At this time there was a powerful Ethiopian colonel. The EPLF wanted to kill him."

Nebiat's friend: "This colonel was really giving the EPLF a hard time. He would go to the battlefield and fill his soldiers with strong fighting morale. When he led a battle the Ethiopian soldiers would fight to the bitter end. He would walk ahead of them, his pistol at the ready, giving them courage. . . . The Ethiopian colonial liked Nebiat. He used to go to her bar and ask when he could meet her. But she always refused because she hated soldiers, especially Ethiopian soldiers."

Nebiat: "The EPLF asked me to help get rid of him. To do my assignment I forced myself and started dating him. He was always very careful; he always had guards around him."

Nebiat's friend: "Nebiat would be called to his car and then taken somewhere. He was always surrounded by Ethiopians; the government was taking special care of him. . . . But with time he started to trust her, [and] he would be in the car in front of the bar but with no guards around him. Sometimes he would take her to his house."

Nebiat: "It took me six months of study to carry out my task."

Nebiat's friend: "One day after he came back from the battlefield he called her on the phone and told her he would send a car to bring her to his house. She went, stayed with him for a while and then said she would like to invite him to her bar for a special welcome, celebrating his success on the battlefield. She told him not to come with his guards and he agreed."

Nebiat: "After this study of six months I succeeded in trapping him in my bar and the fighters liquidated him. I had made all the preparation. I had told the EPLF the time and the place, sold some of my belongings and got my car ready to escape. On Sunday afternoon, he came to my bar and I brought him some drinks. We sat for a while; then I said I would bring a casette and play some music. I went into the bar and told the EPLF men waiting there that everything was ready – they could follow me. They came out and shot him. After that I could not stay on in Asmara. I took my son and I left. I came to the field."

Nebiat's friend: "When she came to the field she was asked if she wanted to go abroad. She answered: 'No, I want to stay and fight with my brothers and sisters.'"

Nebiat: "I had six months' political and military training. I was assigned to the Transport Department where I worked as a mechanic. When Karen was liberated I worked as a driver, transporting people and equipment. Later, in 1981 I was transferred to the Public Administration Department and I have been doing officework in the Central Secretariat since then. My son was 12 when I left. He still keeps contact with his father but he chose to leave with me and he is struggling here with me and I am happy about that.

How has the EPLF affected women's lives? I can see from my own experience how my life has been transformed. More than anything, women can be assertive – and this gives us hope."

5 Fighters

America is the biggest in the world, the king of them all. America hasn't told Mengistu: "Go and fight with guns, artillery trucks if you want to. But don't use planes to destroy the earth." Whenever Mengistu realizes that he is defeated, he kills people with planes. The white kings instead of saying: "These are all our people we will help them"... they see... they keep silent.... Children we gave birth to have disappeared; what we planted has been destroyed. Our houses have been burned. Mengistu knows no justice. The whole world looks on in silence...[24]

Fatna Ari is a resident of Massawa. In a rare programme on British television about the war in Eritrea, the camera caught her and brought us her words of anguish. It was June 1990. The EPLF had captured Massawa. It also held the Asmara–Massawa road and the Ethiopian army was undersiege in Asmara itself.

Ali Haji Abdullahi, an Ethiopian general captured in Massawa, confirmed: "The war is almost over now. The army's morale is low and they don't want to fight.... The central government can't handle it any more unless they start negotiating... they have no other alternative. I don't think they can even last another two or three months."

The bombing of Massawa by the Ethiopian air force still continues, however. The planes go not for the Eritrean People's Liberation Army (EPLA) which is 50 km out of town, but straight to the shanty-town areas where the poorest people live – many of them Ethiopians deliberately settled in this Eritrean city by the Dergue. They bomb them with napalm or with cluster bombs which explode in the air causing untold destruction. The death toll is enormous; whole families have been wiped out. Hundreds are injured, burnt by napalm or trapped under rubble, their limbs torn to shreds by cluster bombs. Aware of the acute shortage of food, the Ethiopian forces have targeted warehouses. 25,000 tons of grain have been destroyed.

Meanwhile Massawa port the point of entry for international food aid in 1984 and after, stands deserted. No government or international agency is willing to use it, partly because of the war and partly because using Massawa as the main point of entry for the whole region would now mean an implicit diplomatic recognition of the EPLF. As Fatna Ari says, "the white kings see but are silent". They have always supported the Ethiopian regime: the United States with its sponsorship of Haile Selassie and later its tolerant help for Mengistu, and after 1978 the Soviet Union which provided arms and military experts to advise the Dergue.

As a result the Western media have never, until vey recently, exposed the nature of the Eritrean struggle. This is compounded by the fact that the left in western countries, particularly Britain, misguidedly and romantically sees the Mengistu regime as socialist. Consequently the 29-year-old struggle, in which a whole generation has grown up, has had little impact on activists in the West. The foremost revolutionary struggle in Africa is simply ignored – its lessons unlearned and its inspiration, which could give us precious sustenance, lost to us.

Operating from this total lack of information, peace activists have asked: "If the EPLF wants peace, why does it go on with the armed struggle?" Askalu Menkarios, the chairperson of the National Union of Eritrean Women (NUEW), told me that she wanted to answer this question and to help people to understand. "We do not want this war, we want peace very much, but the Ethiopians have refused all through to negotiate, and so our desire for peace and our determination to fight for it have to go together. Because really there is no other way of survival . . ." On some occasions, she says, she has been asked in London why the NUEW does not raise issues such as domestic violence. "We say that they are not our issues at the moment. It does not mean that we do not believe in them but that it is not our priority when Ethiopian soldiers are disembowelling Eritrean women."

Askalu talked with me in a low-ceilinged semi-camouflaged room, the office of the NUEW at Hashkerbeb. It was 11 a.m., and outside the rocks all around were radiating a dry, baking heat. Askalu was tired after a long night of travelling and organizational meetings. Her comments about peace and survival are confirmed by the events of Massawa, by the many massacres perpetrated by the Ethiopian, and by the liberated zone with its large number of young disabled women and men who go about their daily tasks on crutches. Like others, they care for children, grow flowers, play music and sing. Many of them were villagers not directly involved in the struggle for freedom. Like Fatna Ari, their bitter experiences tell them that without justice there can never be peace.

Not long after my talk with Askalu I visited the orphanage at Solomona refugee camp. The person in charge was "Abba" Habtomeu – his nickname, "Abba", means father. He was in his thirties. He had been a fighter on the front line till he was seriously injured in 1978. An immensely gentle and caring man, he did not make a fetish of caring. He had been a fighter and now he was doing something just as important: caring for children with the same dedication. He gave me some basic information about the place.

> Wherever you go in Eritrea there are orphans – thousands of orphans. Whenever possible we like to leave them with their relatives. If this is not possible they are sent here by a research team which is in touch with the People's Assemblies in each area. The numbers go up and down with bombardment. Now there are about 500 children, from 2 or 3 months to 7 years old. Very young children are kept with individual staff members. After that they are put in groups – the ostrich group for 2 to 3 year olds; gazelle for 3 to 4; giraffe for 4 to 5 years and elephant for 5 to 6 years. After that they go to the Zero School. The work of the orphanage is divided

into four sections: feeding – previously we gave them spaghetti which was made here, but now it comes from our factory in Orota; washing; psychological section – this develops their thinking through pre-school programmes and helps traumatized children; and finally the clinic, which measures their growth, giving them special foods if they are underweight. . . . The older ones – the 4, 5, and 6 year olds – are the most vulnerable. They remember their parents, they are afraid of sounds, they have bad dreams. They sleep with the staff and the rest of the children of their group. There are always four staff members per dormitory in shifts.

He showed me round. As always when they have visitors, the children came running, they wanted to be touched, to be held, to be kissed. As an American doctor put it: "They are looking for something. The older children communicate that they need parents."

Later "Abba" told me of the raid on Solomona in 1985.

It was on 20th September. Suddenly I heard two Ethiopian pilots talking on FM radio: "It is a good village – I can see civilians running from valley to valley. Choose your target and bomb." They bombed from 9.30 in the morning to 4.30 in the afternoon – cluster bombs and napalm. Thirteen adults and six children were killed. Twenty-four were injured.

There are many questions crucial for an understanding of revolutionary struggle which the Eritrean experience answers. For example, what is the role of violence? Is violence by the oppressed group cathartic, as has been claimed? The Eritrean experience rejects this view completely. As Maaza, a woman cadre I met in Orota and with whom I had a long discussion about the women's movement in the West, told me: "the anger we feel is very strong but we have to learn to channel it, to use it, otherwise it would just destroy us". Underlying this attitude is the history of the EPLF itself from the point of its formation as the result of a struggle within the Eritrean Liberation Front (ELF). This aspect of the EPLF's ideology originated in that struggle. The EPLF rejected the ELF's easy turning of the gun on its own cadres, its killing and silencing of dissidents and its narrow, ethnic chauvinism which made enemies out of those who came as friends (it not only antagonized Christians but excluded and oppressed the Kunamas).

All this was replaced by an approach which identifies the primary contradiction and reserves violence only for the enemy, and deals carefully and sensitively with what Mao calls "contradictions among the people". This means that every possible Eritrean, even the Israeli-trained anti-guerrilla commandos of the Ethiopian army, has been drawn into the struggle on the side of the movement. Ethnic diversity rather than being a source of internal conflict is a source of strength: people are re-educated rather than killed. It also means that the "violence as catharsis" thesis is inevitably rejected because it would involve spontaneous and therefore indiscriminate violence. In the EPLF bases and in the liberated zone as a whole there is intense rejoicing over EPLF victories but it is not because Ethiopians have been killed.

The ultimate demonstration of this is the way in which Ethiopian prisoners of war are treated. There have been thousands of them; in 1990 alone 20,000 were released. They are given medical treatment, food, shelter and basic education. Inevitably they are a strain on Eritrean resources. Incredibly, their food rations are larger that those of Eritrean fighters. When I expressed astonishment I was told that there was a simple, rational reason for this: Ethiopians need and are used to larger amounts of food. Prisoners of war are also taught the history of Eritrea. Many of them, politicized for the first time in their lives, now support the EPLF; some even join it. Haile, who had been taken prisoner in 1979, told me his story:

> I am from the village of Orage in the province of Showa. Orage is also the name of my nationality – our language is Oragnya. My parents were farmers from the middle-farmer level; they owned land and animals. I was sent to Addis to attend school from grade four on inwards, but at the age of 14 I stopped studying because I had no money. I started working, selling books and working in various factories. I was apolitical, neither supporting the government nor opposing it, but at that time there was a war between Ethiopia

and Somalia[25] and people were angry with Somalia so I enlisted. I was 22. In the camp we were given military training and for political training we were told that secessionist bandits were going to take over our land with the help of Arabs. We were sent to Somalia but the war was over so we changed direction and came directly to Eritrea.

Eventually Haile was captured in the fifth offensive.

We had been told that if they capture you they kill you and torture you. But it was the opposite. 500 of us were taken. At that time we were very thirsty. We said: "before you kill us just give us water", but the fighters said: "We'll make you fight the oppressors. We are fighting for the oppressed. Even if you fight us, you are not our enemy." We were kept in one place and given medical treatment. Later we were given political education along with others who were also taught to read and write. We were taught the Eritrean people's real history. For five years I [was] a prisoner, kept under guard. Then I was freed. Some of the freed prisoners joined the TPLF [Tigrayan People's Liberation Front] [and] some the EPDM [Ethiopian People's Democratic Movement]. I chose the EPLF. I decided two or three years ago and joined a year back. At that time 134 other Ethiopian prisoners of war joined the EPLF. We were treated like newcomers to the scene.

For Ethiopian peasants like Haile and other prisoners of war, the experience of being treated with respect by people in authority was a new one. In Ethiopia they had been regarded as expendable cannon-fodder. In May 1976 and again in April 1977, peasants from northern Ethiopia were ordered to march into Eritrea, occupy it and rid it of "rebels". Between twenty and thirty thousands of them were mobilized and driven into Eritrea in government vehicles as part of the so-called Red Peasant Marches. However, as Markakis and Ayele state, "they did not stay long. Forewarned, the Eritrean liberation forces had ample time to prepare a suitable reception. After a few harrassment raids by the Eritreans, the peasants abandoned their camps and wisely fled across the provincial border."[14] Later, from the mid-1980s onwards the minimum age of conscription was reduced. Today's Ethiopian soldiers include boys of 11 and 12, dragged from their mothers, virtually kidnapped by the Ethiopian regime and forced on to the battlefield with little or no training.

The adversary they face now, particularly after the battle of Afabet, is arguably the best equipped army in Africa: its equipment for once has not been donated as aid or even purchased, but captured from the enemy. And arms are not the EPLF's only source of strength, or even its main one. Right from the beginning when the organization was small and ill-equipped, right through the long years of struggle, the EPLF has always relied more on strategy than heavy weaponry, and a brilliant balance of politics and war rather than on brute force.

Who conceived and elaborated these strategies? As usual the EPLF is reluctant to point to any single person. It does not believe in anything which even vaguely resembles or could lead to a personality cult. It considers it more relevant to look at the organization as a whole. What then was the nature of this remarkable fighting force?

Formed by cadres who had sought to transform the ELF and had finally left it, the initial core of the EPLF consisted of three separate groups of fighters, inevitably reflecting ELF structure. The ELF had been organized in five regions: Barka, consisting mainly of Beni-Amer people; Karen, mainly Billen; the Samhar region, representing the Afars; the Sahos; and a mainly Christian Tigrinya group to represent the highlands. The three groups of fighters who re-formed into the EPLF comprised one group from the Barka region, one from the highland region, and a mixed group of fighters from the other regions. The third group had been disarmed because of the turmoil within the ELF and sent to Sudan. From there the fighters went to Aden, entering the field through Danakil. Aden was the point of consolidation of this third group.

Hiwet Ogba Giorgis, who had been a domestic worker in Asmara and had then migrated to Aden to work in 1966, played a key role in this process. She told me about it:

At that time I was not politically conscious. But when I was in Aden I gradually got involved in the Yemeni struggle for liberation. I had experienced the Italians, the British, the Ethiopians, so I felt something for the Yemeni fighters – I cannot tell why but I felt it in my heart and I started helping them. I started contributing monthly to their struggle, cooking for them and taking [food] to their hiding places – I got really involved . . . When they got their independence they gave me a three-storey house in Aden which I later gave to the EPLF.

It was through the Yemenis that the Eritrean fighters heard of me. They asked me to help them because wounded from the field were coming for treatment to Aden. I took care of them, cooked for them and did all the administrative work necessary . . . Once I got involved I stopped working as a domestic. But the Ethiopians got suspicious. They refused to renew my passport because I was "working with rebels", and told all the other Eritrean domestic workers (and there were not that many) to stop speaking to me or they would lose their passports too. I got a Somali passport and I stopped going to Asmara. My friend Haddas Habte who was also a domestic worker refused to obey the Ethiopians and lost her passport too, but she also managed to a get a different one. I would go and see the fighters who had been injured and were in hospital. When they recovered I would bring them to my house, feed them and so on till they were ready to leave for the field.

It was in that period on one unforgettable day [that] I met two Eritrean fighters – Maasho and Tukhu Yihedego. They were from the ELF and they looked very deeply sad. They told us that two of their friends, Woldai Gidai and Kidane Kiflu, had been murdered by the ELF in Kassala . . . for their democratic ideas. Soon after, they and two others, Mesfin Hagos and Mahari Debssai, began to orientate us politically. They explained that we had to start afresh because the ELF couldn't be changed. We had to start something new. They told us to be strong and firm. Tukhu said it was a moment when history was being made. We wrote our names together on a paper and we swore on a candle that we would never betray Eritrea. Tukhu later married my life-long friend Haddas. She now has a son, named Kidane after Kidane Kiflu. Tukhu wanted that child very much but never lived to see him; he too was murdered by the ELF.

In 1970 the EPLF was formed. I had given them my house and it was like a meeting place for those coming from and going to the field. Then in 1971 I was arrested and put in prison for nine months; I still do not know on whose behalf it was done. The Adeni government had been sympathetic to us, but maybe there was a strand within the security who were against us, or maybe it was on behalf of the ELF. For three weeks I was beaten up – slapped so hard that my hearing has been impaired on one side. They asked me: "Do you know the people you are entertaining? Have they got guns? Where do they go?" They asked me about certain specific people, mentioning their names. They threatened to kill me if I did not tell them. I said: "I don't know anything about politics; I just help them because they are Eritreans". At that time the Ethiopians intervened, saying that I should not be detained and that they would look after me. Of course they had refused me a passport, so "looking after" me probably meant trying to kill me. Eventually the EPLF intervened – they were strong and well-established by then, and they approached the number-two man in the government and I was released. I carried on my work in Aden, and later also co-ordinated the care of the wounded in Beirut and Syria.

During these early days the EPLF's essential political form and outlook developed. As Ande Michael Kahsai explained:

There was the question of bringing together the three groups which made up the EPLF, and giving political education which would make us think of ourselves as a nation. It was an extremely crucial period, when people started having a common vision. It was because of this that despite all the material difficulties the organization could survive. It was a small organization but we had cohesion. That is why, in 1974 when we started getting a flood of new people – 200 a day from Asmara alone – and when the danger was not only that we would not be able to arm them but that we would lose our political balance, we maintained the same politics.

In 1973, among the hundreds of new members were the first four women. One of them was Worku Zerai. She told me about the nature of the group she joined and the attitudes to women.

I joined the armed struggle some 11km north of Asmara. From there we came to Sahel and after 15 days were assigned to the fighting force like everyone else – in those days there was no base area so some were trained on assignment.

The first four women who joined were all students, three from Addis and one from Asmara. We were welcomed very much by the fighters. But they were very shy with us. They used to pity us because we were women. Everyone was helpful and encouraging. When we were doing our military training, some did not believe that we could do it. Some would hide and see if we could do it. We were not allowed to do cooking. Normally everyone does it, but out of consideration for us we were asked not to.

I was very happy. What impressed me was the composition of the EPLF: peasants, high-school students, university students, but I was surprised because I had not known how small the EPLF was. Books mislead you. I had read about Guinea Bissau and Mozambique, and I thought it might be something like that. But the EPLF – my group was 500 men!

What impressed me too was the political education we were given, and the way people received it, and their comradeship. This comradeship was reflected in the way they worked. If one goes to bring water, everyone tries to go. In the battle everyone wants to go. Everyone wants to teach you, inform you. I myself was surprised how quickly I got integrated into this society. It was not a conscious or deliberate integration . . . Some Marxist books say peasants are barbarians. I found peasants to be very human. In a short time you find yourself defending the EPLF. In the first, second, third week I used to say "you" but then I started saying "we" – I don't know how it happened.

At that time transportation was by camel (this went on till 1975). We used to walk but if you wanted to transport food you would use a camel. A fighter would go in front leading the camel. If we saw such a caravan we would run to them, take the rope and the gun of the fighter, tell him to sit, and bring him food and water. Then we would unload the camel and take the provisions to the store. It is the idea that all work belongs to all of you. The revolution belongs to all of you. You are all equally responsible. When they see a battle everyone takes their belt and gun and wants to fight. No one wants to be left behind. This culture has been maintained up to now – this is what makes the EPLF what it is. You want to sacrifice yourself and bring something good to the people, and even among those who sacrifice themselves, everyone wants to be the first. You develop a kind of selflessness.

At that time most of us were very young, teenagers or in our early twenties. Most of the present EPLF leadership comes from that generation. Those who had come from the ELF were perhaps more mature; they include Ramadan [Secretary General of the EPLF till 1987] and Issayus [current Secretary General of the EPLF] . . . . I was on the front line for six months but at that time there were no attacks – I was unlucky.

Underlying Worku's account of the comradeship, selflessness and love which support every fighter are two important aspects of the fighting force. First, although there are leaders there is no two-tier system, no "officers and other ranks"; and second, it was established from the beginning that every single member of the Front would have to undergo political and military training, after which he or she would be assigned to a particular area of work. Worku and many others also stressed the importance given to political education, and education in general. The approach that education is an essential part of life is characteristic of the EPLF. In all the liberated areas, in all kinds of situations, people are learning and teaching. Patients recovering in hospitals become literate; fighters learn new non-military skills as they relax; traditional midwives learn how to use modern medical instruments; and housewives learn how to farm. In addition there is the more conventional education programme for the country as a whole (outlined in Appendix 2).

Once a base area had been secured, the EPLF was able to organize itself better. As far as women were concerned, as the months passed more women joined the movement, and this in itself served to alter male attitudes. By 1977 there were hundreds of women in the EPLF. Chu chu, whom I know only by her nickname, joined that year. She gave me a detailed account both of the training received by those who joined, and the attitudes of male cadres to women:

> In 1977 the Ethiopian government was saying: "the Eritrean bandits are very few, they are useless, they have nothing to eat or drink, we can destroy them within two days . . ." But when I joined, I found 400 women in the training school. I was surprised; I cried because I was so happy to see the number of women who had come to join. There were a few from abroad, from America; and a few from Ethiopia: students, peasants and factory workers.
>
> The training is very hard at the beginning. You have to get up early, you have to run. . . . I found it easier than many others because I come from a village – Gamugofa in Ethiopia (although I am an Eritrean). Gamugofa is very backward and people there really have to work hard physically. They have to carry water a long way and grind grain by hand. That background helped me in my training . . . but in general in Eritrea, because it is a feudo-capitalist society, women do not traditionally develop their physical strength. They do not for example play tennis or volleyball, so it takes time to develop [their] physique. This was why women are given six months' training and men get three. But after the training there is no difference – on the front line men and women are the same.
>
> The women were all ages from about 16 to 40 or 45. There were women who had come with their children. The children could be as old as 18 or 20 and the mothers 40 or 45. For all these women it was the first experience of running and exercise. The political education is about Eritrean history. People only come with their own experience – every Eritrean has lost a mother or father or sister or brother – but they have to know why they are struggling, what is the history, why we say Eritrea is a country. The women are taught to practise so that they can do what men can do. Because it is better, more convincing, to practise than just to learn it in theory. That is the principle of the EPLF.
>
> After six months [women] are assigned to a particular job – some go to hospitals, some are teachers, some go to garages, some to the front line. So now we have a woman company commander: she does

not command only women, but men and women. At least 200 men are under her. There are many women company commanders, squad commanders and platoon commanders. This is not done just for the sake of rights for women but because Eritreans are fighting for freedom, and to fight for freedom you have to have your rights.

When the first women joined in 1973, the men thought. "What can they do, these women." Then the men saw what women could do – in the clinics and as dressers and at the front line. They saw them fight, take prisoners, capture tanks; they saw them when they lost their legs, their eyes. Then they stopped speaking about women, now they accept women.

By January 1977, the EPLF had held its first Organizational Congress which adopted a National Democratic Programme (see Appendix 1). Its 11 objectives were: to establish a people's democratic state; to build an independent, self-reliant and planned national economy; to develop culture, education, technology and public health; to safeguard social rights; to ensure the quality and consolidate the unity of nationalities; to build a strong people's army; to respect freedom of religion and faith; provide humane treatment for prisoners of war and encourage the desertion of Eritrean soldiers serving the enemy; to protect the rights of Eritreans living abroad; to respect the rights of foreigners residing in Eritrea; and to pursue a common policy of peace and non-alignment.

These objectives were already being pursued but the Congress formalized them. In addition it formulated a military strategy for the next phase. It was obviously the right one because it was followed by a remarkable series of victories: Nacfa, Afabet, Decemhare, Karen, Segeneiti and Digaa were all liberated between March and August 1977. After that the crucial Massawa–Asmara highway, currently being held by the EPLF, came under its control for the first time. More victories followed – Dogali, parts of Massawa, Dongolo, Ginda, Embatkala, Maihabar, Nafasit and Seidici. At the same time the ELF liberated Tessenei, Agordat, Mendafera and Adi Qula, and laid siege to Barentu. Liberation of Eritrea seemed within reach when the Soviet Union intervened with massive arms aid to Ethiopia.

Asmeret Abraham, well known in the EPLF as a brilliant organizer behind the enemy lines (see p.74) and as a heroic fighter (she is nicknamed Gwandi after a type of gun), took part in the battles of this phase and told me briefly about them.

> After I finished my military training and political education, I was assigned to the fighting forces, fighting round Asmara in Karnishun district. In 1975 there were battles almost every month on the Asmara–Karen road. I participated in them, and was involved in the siege of Nacfa in 1977 and the battle of Afabet the same year. . . . I have participated in more than fifty battles . . .

Then she grew silent and Worku took over.

> She played a heroic role in the battle of Adaie. It was the turning point, because we had been capturing one town after another but here the Ethiopians had Soviet arms! Gwandi was a squadron leader. A lot of her comrades were being wounded and martyred. At a certain point her company leader was also martyred. She took control and led the whole company. She was taking orders from the battalion commander. She got wounded in the hand but rather than go to the hospital she just bandaged the wound and continued. Then the battalion leader was also wounded. She took his place and started leading the whole battalion. She continued the battle until she was ordered to retreat with her soldiers. Her actions prevented the EPLF from total surrender in this battle.

Gwandi told me that until the battle of Adaie the strength of the people's army and the people's militia was at a peak, but they were now faced by the formidable military power delivered by the Soviet Union. The EPLF could not immediately defend all the land which it had liberated. A policy of strategic withdrawal was decided upon, which avoided immediate confrontation and thus prevented civilian and military casualties.

This was the beginning of a new phase similar to that which occurred in China between June 1946 and September 1947.[26] It signified a war of self-defence with a policy of strategic defensive and tactical offensive, and allowed the EPLF to avoid civilian and military casualties, while:

conserving weapons, inflicting manpower, material and morale losses on the enemy, and, what is more, increasing your fire power, maintaining and boosting your morale, protecting institutions from destruction so they could later be used for reconstruction and the inevitable counter offensive . . .

It also made it possible for the EPLF to evacuate towns and remove equipment to the base areas, and to confront the Ethiopians at places of their own choice. Most crucially, it confirmed the importance which the EPLF placed in base areas.

This phase inevitably had its negative effects, however. The economic and social changes initiated in those liberated areas now taken over by the Ethiopians had to be more or less suspended. The strategic withdrawal also meant the physical separation of the most densely populated areas from the EPLF. This is reflected in the very different political consciousness of refugees who left these densely populated areas in recent years compared with those who left before or around 1978.

The next few years consisted of two distinct military phases. First, during the period between July 1978 and April 1979 the Ethiopians launched four offensives while the EPLA retreated gradually to its fortifications. This cost the Ethiopians 25,000 men and a considerable loss of equipment which was taken over by the Eritreans. Gwandi was injured in the leg in the fourth of these offensives but she was treated and recovered. The fifth Ethiopian offensive in July 1979 and was part of the second phase, when the Ethiopians tried to encircle the EPLA and breach its defences. After careful preparations and reinforcements of troops the Ethiopians advanced towards Agrae while simultaneously and continuously attacking on all fronts. However, they suffered an enormous defeat losing 12,000 soldiers and a substantial amount of military equipment. Gwandi was wounded again in this offensive, in the right side of her chest. Once more she returned after treatment and took part in the EPLA counter-offensive which drove the Ethiopian army from the Nacfa front and consolidated defences. But the wound in her chest had not healed properly, and she was taken out of the fighting force and assigned to the Department of

Public Administration. From there she was sent again to work behind the enemy lines in Asmara.

The fifth offensive was followed by a period of nearly three years during which the Dergue prepared itself for another massive onslaught: the Red Star Campaign, the sixth offensive whose aim was to wipe out the EPLF in a two- to three-week war of encirclement. As a prelude the Dergue started a political and propaganda campaign in Eritrea to try to demoralize the Eritrean people. This was followed in December 1981 by a combing campaign behind the enemy lines, and then a month of intensive bombing in the whole region when thousands of civilians were killed and foods stores, houses, schools and other targets were destroyed. On 15 February 1982 the main attack came, on three fronts: north-east Sahel, Nacfa and Kerkebet (Barka). The third Ethiopian front was comparatively new and collapsed within a few days, but on the other two fronts heavy fighting continued for more than three months and finally ended in a massive defeat for the Dergue. Forty thousand Ethiopian soldiers were killed.

The sixth offensive has been described by the EPLF as "a valuable military experience in which it surmounted a difficult and trying stage". It is also remembered as a time of great suffering for the civilian population, when, as Worku Zerai said:

> We were again made aware of the Dergue's genocidal intentions. The days of bombardment were terrible. The bombing went on and on. When they start bombing an area you feel completely exposed because you can hear the pilots talking on FM radio: "Look, there is a food store! Target that!" or: "Look, that looks like a school, hit that!" They used napalm and cluster bombs. The effect of cluster bombs, because they explode in the air, is to destroy everything completely, tearing everything to tiny shreds. Once some comrades and I heard the pilots talking on the radio. They had seen a flock of goats which they mistook for civilians. We took cover underground and escaped. Later we found the place strewn with what had been the goats – eyes, bits of skin, hoofs . . .

Even under these conditions the EPLF used the period of the sixth offensive for further consolidation. For example, this was when the Central Hospital was moved to Orota, a base strategically located for safety. The setting up of people's assemblies and branches of the mass organizations, land redistribution programmes, changes in marriage laws, and education and health schemes not only went on right through this period but actually gathered momentum. Thus the year from 1977 onwards were a time when the infrastructure of the modern Eritrean nation, already partly in place, was being further developed and consolidated.

As we have seen, in the mid-1970s the Dergue had dismantled and transported whole factories from Eritrean towns to Addis Ababa. This resulted in large numbers of skilled workers joining liberation movements. By 1977 the EPLF and ELF between them controlled most of Eritrea except Asmara. In the towns under its control the EPLF managed to get power-stations running, and telephone communications and water supplies working. Simultaneously it began to expand light industries in the liberated zone by transporting essential machinery from the towns. In 1977-8 alone the number of skilled workers in the EPLF increased three-fold and millions of pounds worth of materials were being manufactured. This was part of the EPLF's economic strategy to fulfil one of its main objectives: self-reliance. As the EPLF states:

> In an economically backward third world country like Eritrea given the domination of world markets by the imperialist countries, this policy of self reliance is a necessary precondition for the establishment of an independent and developed economy. The pursuance of a policy of self reliance is essential for the total independence and liberation of society. Politically it is the only means to complete freedom. Economically it is likewise the only means . . . socially it is an essentially liberating process emphasising as it does working cooperatively and collectively to satisfy your own needs. Dependence breeds subservience and lack of self-confidence.[27]

These developments, far beyond what most countries in the Third World have achieved in peacetime, have not only occured in the course of this painful and protracted war but are, in many cases, an integral part of the armed struggle. The needs and demands of the armed struggle have led to developments in industry which in turn have pushed the struggle ahead. For example, women fighters' essential need for sanitary towels led not to charity collections in the West, as has been the case with many other liberation movements, but to the NUEW raising funds and then buying and installing a machine to produce sanitary towels in the liberated zone. It is now proudly displayed to visitors. On another level and another scale, the "Challenge Road," a highway through steep mountains with 37 hairpin bends, a tremendous feat of modern engineering was built in 1982 to give access to the north-east Sahel front.

At the same time, with the EPLF's ability to find something potentially useful in every situation, the discarded hardware of the war has been the springboard for further developments. While generators, mobile garages and metal and wood-working machines have been acquired from the enemy in course of the war, things are also constantly adapted and recycled. Trucks are being converted into oil – and water-carriers. Machines which build other machines are being built out of the wrecks of yet other machines. A variety of items, from cooking utensils to hospital equipment, are made out of the metal and wooden debris of war. As James Firebrace and Stuart Holland wrote after their trip to the liberated zone in 1984: "From our own observations the most useful materials are the wood from ammunition boxes, shell and bomb casings, springs and sheet metal from destroyed vehicles. The process is almost literally from shells to ploughshares."[28]

What is immediately apparent is a brilliant model for development. Underlying it is something even more unique and striking: a remarkable energy and dynamism and creativity, as though some spring has been tapped which lies dormant in human beings elsewhere. Perhaps it is partly the result of a commitment which becomes stronger when the people collectively do what they are convinced is in their interests, and partly the result of the specific Eritrean experience. As the EPLF states:

Not only has so much work been done relying on our fighters and organised masses, but a rich experience and confidence in organised collective work, a new awareness and confidence in being able to accomplish feats of amazing and ingenious work relying on one's own determined and organised effort, and an understanding of the fact that the best and quickest results could be achieved through voluntary collective work has also been gained. The long term effect of this new awareness and confidence is most important, for it will be essential in the struggle to come to reconstruct and develop our economy, to lay the base for a developed socialist society.[27]

From 1978 onwards the Soviet Union continued to support Ethiopia, giving it vast amounts of military aid and even sending over military experts to advise the Ethiopian forces on the spot. But it was all to no avail, and large amounts of Soviet military hardware ended up in Eritrean hands. Meanwhile Mengistu's paranoia and self-deception had reached gigantic proportions. To add to his problems there were intense conflicts within the Ethiopian armed forces, settled invariably by executions.

In this situation the Dergue assessed the sixth offensive as a success, despite the 40,000 casualties it had suffered. It decided to follow it up with the "final attack" on the EPLF. In March 1983 it launched the seventh offensive, also known as the "Stealth Offensive". Unlike the sixth offensive, this time there was no fanfare, and while previously the Ethiopians attacked on all fronts at the same time, they now attacked on one front and then shifted to another. Once again they were defeated. The next phase of military strategy was one of EPLA counter – offensives. At the beginning of 1984, Tessenei and Alighider were taken. In March the Dergue was dislodged from the north-east Sahel front where it had been entrenched for five years, and a considerable area of the countryside was liberated. Then in July 1985, after a dramatic battle in which the Ethiopian army suffered heavy losses, the EPLA took Barentu. The Dergue then went all out, bringing in many additional brigades and its biggest mechanized division from the Ogaden.[25] It eventually recaptured Barentu and also Tessenei in the last week of August.

In October, having reinforced itself with a new batch of 20,000 conscripts, the Dergue launched a new large-scale offensive which was advertised as the one which would eliminate the EPLF in a week. The soldiers were deeply demoralized, however. For some years they had been deserting in large numbers, and by now were surrendering at a rate of seven per day. Not surprisingly, this offensive too turned out to be another crushing defeat for the Ethiopians. It brought this particular phase of the military struggle to an end because while skirmishes continued there were no more offensives from the Dergue. It was clear that from now on the EPLF held the initiative.

The EPLF did not launch any attacks immediately, however. Instead, it further strengthened itself by finally achieving unity with the leadership of the only remaining wing of the ELF of any significance (see Appendix 3 for divisions in the ELF after 1981). This was formalized in the Unity Congress of May 1987. Then, as many times in the past, the EPLF once again proposed a political solution to the conflict. This time a truce was suggested, to be followed by a referendum supervised by the United Nations, the Organization of African Unity, the Non-aligned movement or the Arab League, in which the Eritrean population would be asked to choose between independence, federation with Ethiopia or regional autonomy.

The Ethiopians refused, and were exposed to the Eritrean people and to the world as unwilling to accept a peaceful (and even face-saving) way out of the conflict in which so many had lost their lives. This created political support among the Eritrean people which was a precondition for the general offensive which was to follow.

The new phase started in December 1987, when the EPLA attacked one side of the Nacfa front and delivered a crushing defeat. The situation is best understood by studying the battles of 17, 18 and 19 March 1988 when the EPLA finally obliterated the Nacfa front and took the town of Afabet. Since the strategic retreat ten years before the main arena of trench warfare, had extended for 120 km in a maze of underground bunkers, from the hills of Habero and Rora Habab to western Afabet and eastern Nacfa through to Aaget, Felket and Ketan north of

Afabet. The small town of Afabet was the main headquarters of the Ethiopian High Command for the entire front, and the main military depot for the divisions deployed, and the centre of army intelligence. From here the Ethiopians had during the previous ten years planned their strategic objective of penetrating the EPLF's base areas.

The battles in March brought a victory which was unprecedented in its scale and significance. It wiped out one third of the Ethiopian army in Eritrea and captured an incredible array of weapons: tanks; over a hundred military vehicles; 60 cannons of different types; and 20 anti-aircraft guns. In addition it demolished the Ethiopian High Command, and captured three Soviet advisors (two colonels and one lieutenant) as well as thousands of soldiers. The scale of the victory has been compared to that in Dien Ben Phu in 1954.

I was able to visit Afabet a year after this historic battle. Travelling at night as always, we approached it from the cool Rora highlands, traversing what appeared to be endless river-beds and then entering new mountains at whose heart our destination lay. I had heard of the battle of Afabet but it was still a shock when we turned a bend and saw in the glare of the headlights the huge wreck of a tank lying by the road side. Then there were more and more tanks, and rocket-launchers, huge guns and many other types of military equipment – misshapen and rusted, thrown in the bushes. They were chilling evidence of the nature of the Ethiopian attack, though my companions told me thy represented only a fraction of the Ethiopian onslaught as the rest had been cleared away. Now they were all that remained of the elite corps of the Ethiopian army. During the sixth offensive, I was told, the Ethiopians had come with three kinds of soldiers:

> those in the north-eastern front, the Waquao (which means "beat them"); those through Barka, the Mebrek which means "a sudden attack like thunder" . . . and the Nados who came through the Nacfa front. The Mebrek were eliminated in the sixth offensive, and the Waquao in the north-eastern front in 1984. The Nados, 20,000 highly arrogant men with very sophisticated weapons they

thought they were invincible – were finished in Afabet. . . . This huge convoy of vehicles, including Stalin organs and led by a tank, was moving along this road towards Afabet. The EPLA tanks were hidden in the mountains. They ambushed the first tank in a pass and immobilized it. And this immobilized the entire convoy. The EPLA then simply attacked them one by one with no losses to themselves.

The town of Afabet seemed very quiet as we entered it. Right next to it was the Ethiopian military base and the house where the commander had lived. It had luxury fittings: a western-style toilet which was close with barbed wire, and a built-in bar where the commander had entertained his Soviet guests. The place had a smell of corruption and cruelty about it. Near it were trenches and piles of ammunition, again only a fraction of what the EPLF had recovered.

Morning dawned, the hills appeared blue-grey in colour and I could see the town in their centre. It was a white-washed market town with small shops supplying the area, and a small public square named Red Square. Sitting incongruously between the military base and the town was a sign with the hammer and sickle on it; underneath in Amaharic was the slogan: "Revolution or death".

Afabet had an air of cautiously returning to life and this was confirmed by many of the women we met. One of them was Saida Mandar, a Muslim of Tigre nationality like the majority of the population here. She told me about the years of Ethiopian occupation:

> Our life here has been terrible . . . it was just humiliation, torture and killing. And if we went out of the town they would not let us back in. So we went on living here because we prefer to live a terrible life here to leaving. . . . Here, no woman was safe. We lived in fear of rape. It was very common and many of us have been forced to bear the children of Ethiopian Soldiers. They used all kinds of pretexts to attack us sexually. They would ask us to go to meetings or classes and try to abuse us there, and in the base they had women servants whom they used as prostitutes.
>
> This town has been captured three times. When the EPLF took it the first time most people ran away. The EPLF told us: "Come

back! This is your town; give us directives about what you want." After a week everyone came back. The Ethiopians when they came – they would not allow us access even to drinking water. They made no-go areas in the town; anyone who went there was killed and their relatives were not allowed to bury their bodies. It is only now that some of those burials are taking place.

This time the battle of Afabet started at 6 a.m. There was bombardment by heavy artillery. No one went out. We locked our houses; only occasionally we would go and peep out to see what was going on. Around 5.30 or 6 p.m. the Ethiopians started to burn their own stores and run away. By 7.30 it was all very quiet. We crept out – we could not believe our eyes. The Ethiopians were all gone, the trenches empty, the ammunition everywhere and EPLF soldiers running here and there. We ran out to greet them and feed them. We never thought the Ethiopians would go, – the number of soldiers they had! – the type of ammunition they had!

The atmosphere in Afabet when it was liberated, with the rejoicing of the people, has been captured by the EPLF photographic crew who follow every battle. In the remarkable film of this most crucial revolutionary battle one can see strategy being put into practice and feel the moment when the fighters, men and women, and the people's militia unite to make history.

Mengistu's response to his crushing defeat in Afabet was swift, brutal and predictable. As Fatna Ari from Massawa said: "Whenever he is defeated he kills civilians." The village of She'eb in Semhar was chosen as a target. What happened there is related by Amna Mohamed Shembera, a woman who survived the massacre and fled to the liberated zone with her two babies and four other small children:

At 8.00 in the morning on May 12, about 15 Ethiopian tanks came from the direction of Mai Awalid and surrounded She'eb. Some of us tried to flee but were turned back and told to attend a "meeting". In fact we were herded into a small dugout under a tree where we were crushed by tanks that rolled over our bodies again and again. Then they turned their guns on us and started shooting and killing those who were not already crushed to death . . . Then the Ethiopian soldiers started snatching jewellery and other valuables off the corpses and then moved on to burn houses . . . I pretended to be dead and when the killers moved further away I pulled my two children and four others, including Amna Adem who was shot in the back, closer to me. I covered them with blood-soaked sheets from the corpses and told them to lie low. . . . The third night after the attack we fled westwards.[29]

As we wait to see whether Mengistu might at last come to his senses and decide on negotiation, the TPLF is closing in on Addis Ababa. His days are numbered. He will be remembered by the people of Ethiopia for no positive or constructive achievement but for his cruelty, ruthlessness, his subservience to the Soviet Union and his gigantic personal ego.

6 Land Reform

All through the stormy and tortured years of the war, a process of reform of land ownership and marriage laws has been taking place in the liberated areas. In terms of affecting women's position, the two transformations are closely interlinked. The fact that women did not traditionally own land meant that they had no control over the only means of production, let alone over the products of their labour. This economic powerlessness was reflected within the family and was institutionalized in the rules of marriage. The processes of change occurred quite independently of each other, however, and to understand them it is necessary to look at them separately.

Traditional land ownership in Eritrea is extremely complex. In very broad terms, two types of land can be identified. First, there are the highlands with settled agriculture and high population density; the people are mainly Tigrinya-speaking Christians. Second, there are the desert lowlands which are more sparsely populated and where the population consists of a number of ethnic nationalities: the nomadic or semi-nomadic pastoralist Muslims who speak Tigre (the largest group in the lowlands); the nomadic Muslim Rashaidas; and the settled agriculturalists – the mainly animist Kunamas and the Naras who recently converted from animism to Islam. In both the highlands and the lowlands there are essentially four types of landholding, although each has many regional variations and some are far more common in one part of the country than in another. They are: private ownership, family ownership, village ownership, and *dominiale* or state land.

In the highland villages individual ownership and family ownership are both common; they are called *tselmi* and *resti* respectively. In *tselmi*, when a man dies his land is divided among male descendants, and in *resti* it passes back to the collective hereditary plot. In neither case do women have rights to land, and nor does a group called the Makelai Aliet. The latter group comprises people who, although they may have lived in the village for generations, are regarded as outsiders and second-class citizens.[30] Possessing hereditary land (or being a *restinya*) is regarded traditionally as having something akin to a sacred right over land, and hereditary power. That this society has certain strong elements of early feudalism is demonstrated by the obligations and privileges which go with *resti*: it is the *restinya* who is in charge of all communal labour, the care of the church and all other administrative and political duties. Women, even of the powerful *endas*,[31] are excluded from all these duties and all public life.

Collective village ownership, *diesa*, in the highlands is of recent origin. Here it represents a compromise to pacify the conflicts caused by the intense pressure on land exacerbated by the continued sub-division of plots under the *tselmi* system of inheritance. Unlike village ownership in the lowland Nara and Kunama areas which are a part of the communal co-operative system of agriculture going back hundreds of years, in the highlands much of the *diesa* land originated in the Italian period. At that time appropriation of land for plantations, airports and roads led to intense shortages of land for subsistence farming. The Italians tried to pacify the poor peasants by offering this compromise while at the same time maintaining the status and power of the *restinya* by putting them in charge of land redistribution. As a result, highland village ownership systems are far from egalitarian. Not surprisingly, the position of women under the *diesa* system is no different from that under private or family ownership.

In the lowlands there are many different social formations. The second largest ethnic group, the Tigre speakers, comprise clans which come together in tribes. But whereas in the highlands the clans or *endas* coexist within an unequal land ownership system (where some clans own far more than others of the same size and are therefore more powerful and prestigious), in these lowland groups the clans are organized into two main tribes which have a relationship of dominance and servitude. Thus, for example, the Beni Amer confederation of tribes, living mainly in the Barka region of the western lowlands, is divided into the Nabtab ("aristocrats") and the Hdreb ("serfs").[32] The Habab tribes, who live in the Sahel area, consist of the Asgede and Shumgele "aristocrats", who dominate the Tigre and Beja "serfs".

This can be seen more clearly at ground level by looking once again at the town of Afabet where, despite the war, the Eritrean People's Liberation Front (EPLF) implemented land reform from 1977 onwards. The people living in and near the town are mainly Tigre-speaking Muslims, both "serfs" and "aristocrats" from the Habab clan. Like Fatma Omer and her family (p.39), they are semi-nomadic agricultural pastoralists who spend six months in the highlands and six months, in this area, settling mainly in the countryside around Arabet from June to November, during the highland rainy season.

In the nineteenth century the Habab aristocrats were described as being immensely wealthy,[33] but their wealth even then did not come from a self-sufficient or integrated economy. They are said to have traded their livestock in Sudan and their butter in Arabia via Massawa. After the Italians took control of much of the lowland area as *dominiale* land in 1909, it was given over as concession land to the Habab. This was the case in Wadi Labca, the area which spans the valley of the Labca from the Red Sea to near Afabet. Here, particularly in the mouth of the Labca, the clan constructed an irrigation system and both serfs and aristocrats had plots of land. However, the serfs' plots were not large enough to support them and so they also had to work on the aristocrats' land to make ends meet. Payment took the form of either a cash wage or grain. There were also serfs who did not own any land; they too worked on the aristocrats' land in exchange for a small plot for themselves. The aristocrats, with rights to the largest plots of land, administered the area and organized the labour. The land required constant careful tending: during the winter months the irrigation system had to be repaired, the land ploughed and winter crops sown and harvested; and in the summer millet, the main crop, was sown.

The area exhibited a wide variety of relations of production – from remnants of slavery,[34] tribal cultivation and pastoralism, through essentially feudal relations, to wage labour. These were set within a variety of rules which signified a hierarchical relationship between the tribes who made up the Habab. For example, whenever a feudal lord met with a serf by coincidence, the former reserved the right to demand one Maria Therese thaler.[35] During the drought, when cattle give the least amount of milk, the serf was obliged to provide his lord with meat. In areas administered by the Bet Asgede, the feudal lord had a right to one cow and 16 tins of butter from the serfs, and a quarter of the produce of farmers. These oppressive relations had led to a series of uprisings.

As the EPLF stated in describing the situation confronting it when it started work in the area in 1975:

> Feudal oppression by the Lords of the Bet Asgede continued without any change or reform even during British rule. Thus from 1942 to 49, 200,000 serfs rose in rebellion and Wadi Labca served as the centre of the rebellion. Although this movement weakened the political power of the feudal lords and the institution of serfdom, the feudal chiefs of Ad-Temariam still retained the power to buy and control dominiale land. This meant that particularly that portion of the land which could be easily irrigated remained in the hands of the feudal chiefs.
>
> Dominiale land was divided among the tribes, such that the stronger tribes took the largest and best plots, whereas less powerful tribes had to be content with dividing the rest of the land. In the distribution of tribal land, the best and largest plots were taken by the feudal chiefs, in the order of their hierarchal position on the administrative ladder. It was land left over from this that was shared by the people.
>
> This system of redistribution and administration of land continued throughout the federal period and the formal colonisation of Eritrea by the Haile Selassie regime. Worse still in the early seventies, the

feudal chiefs of Ad-Temariam even started to sell dominiale land to those who are able to put up money for it.[36]

Within this economic framework, what was the position of women? I posed the question to two women from this region. The first was Fatma Omer, who spoke to me in the Rora mountain area where her family have now permanently settled, linked to one of the EPLF's development projects.

> My parents have land here, 5 tsimdis of land; 5 tsimdis is about average. We used to grow millet, wheat, barley and other cereals and we also had cows and goats. My father used to plough, we did not employ workers. We used to spend three to four months of the year in the lowlands. My mother died after she gave birth to four boys and three girls. Three of the boys died. My father then married again.
>
> I was 15 when my mother died. I used to help my father in the fields. The women in our village, they do most jobs except cutting the harvest and even that is not a taboo. I used to help with the weeding, pounding, collecting the harvest and of course the household work.
>
> For the woman the hardest time of the year is when the family go to the lowlands. First she has to dismantle the tent in front of her house and loads it on to an ox or donkey. Then she gets the ready and attends to the children and goats, and then place the kitchen utensils on the donkey. Every time they stop on the journey, it is the woman's duty to set up the tent, prepare food and look after the children and goats. The man comes in the tent and sleeps. She makes porridge and coffee and feeds him. He eats, sometimes alone, sometimes with his children. If he leaves anything, the woman eats. During the night they move again – the same process all over again. It takes ten days to go to the lowlands [of Sahel] . . . The best food, the best clothes, the best bed are for the man.
>
> I was infibulated and circumcised; it is our traditional culture. They say it is bad if a girl is not infibulated.
>
> I was married at fifteen. It was arranged by my parents. I did not know even what colour he was. I was trying to see him peeping through my veil. I was very shy.

(Here Fatma was talking about the Rora Bagla area where many of the people are semi-nomadic, spending the summer in the lowlands).

Underlying this oppression is women's total powerlessness, caused by their lack of any control over the means of production: land. In such a society, changing the pattern of land ownership is a fundamental transformation which both enables and secures social and ideological changes. Giving land to women in a society where they never owned it before creates a profound upheaval, not only because land is being given to women, with all the inherent ideological implications, but because land becomes accessible to a previously excluded 50% of the population. The broad aims of the EPLF's land reform programme lie within this upheaval. They do not at this stage attempt to create socialist relations of production, but aim to destroy the feudal forms of production, to build a new and equitable base, and to increase output. Not only is Eritrea short of food, but the EPLF's aim of developing a strong industrial sector requires the rapid development of productive forces in agriculture. The EPLF's concept of balanced development like that adopted in China under Mao implies that the agricultural sector not only provides inputs for the industrial sector (both food and raw materials) and a market for industrial producer goods (farm machinery etc.) but also a market for industrial consumer goods. Developing the production of mass consumer goods is in turn linked to the goal of improving the overall standard of living of the peasantry.

While increasing agricultural output is an extremely difficult task in any country, it is particularly so in Eritrea. Here the whole subject of land reform was one of which the masses were extremely wary. Over the decades they had had many different forms of land alienation and punitive land redistribution imposed upon them, often in the name of reform. They remembered the Italians and their land robbery, which was followed by an attempt to pacify them by converting *tselmi* to *diesa*, or bits of *dominiale* to "concession" land – a change which left land redistribution in the hands of the rich landowning families and as such did not really improve the situation of the poor. They remembered too the period of British rule when land hunger was acute in both the highlands and the lowlands, and major struggles were undertaken by the "serfs" in Barka and Sahel, only to be crushed by the authorities. Ethiopian activities in this field are fresh in their minds: the handing over of fertile land, to the Americans for military bases and installations, and to foreign multinationals like Baratolo. Not surprisingly the peasantry in general hated the very thought of land redistribution.

Here as elsewhere the EPLF used its general policy of laying down methods of work from above, while simultaneously working from the concrete experiences of the people in putting these aims and methods into practice. But it was in this "working from below" that Wadi Labca presented specific problems. The area had been influenced by the Eritrean Liberation Front (ELF) but not very deeply. When the EPLF arrived on the scene, the feudal lords, impressed by the EPLF's achievements and its medical services, at first extended a hand of friendship to the organization. Meanwhile the peasants told of their suffering at the hands of the ELF, but it took them some time to assess the political nature of the EPLF. The reason for this "period of transition", after which they began to raise issues such as demands for land with the EPLF, is interesting. The EPLF interprets it as one of the effects of being viewed initially by the population not as a "political organisation carrying out armed struggle but as a military organisation". The EPLF then started, as always when embarking on this kind of task, to create what it saw as essential preconditions.

First, the economic conditions and relations of the area had to be studied in depth in order to estimate the balance of forces for and against land redistribution. The lords of this area were not only powerful in themselves but had the support of their counterparts from Karen and Nacfa. Second, the poor peasants and serfs had to be made to realize the aims of this particular struggle, and their role and position in it. This was not easy. It required an understanding of the way the priests, both Christain and Muslim, constantly reinforced the power structures: for example by sanctioning the view that taking another person's land was prohibited by the Koran and was likely to lead to a worse life in the "other world". It also require the politicization of people who had very little free time for political meetings because of the intense exploitation they faced; and who over the generations had been taught to suppress their deep hatred for their oppressors on whom they were economically dependent.

As the EPLF summarizes:

> Economic insecurity, cultural backwardness, illiteracy, the peasant's unabating bulk of work, cruel exploitation, along with the subtle influences of the religious and spiritual world, had such an effect on the mentality of the peasants that the technique to be applied in the process of political education and dialogue with the masses was bound to be problematic, long, repetitive and demanding of great patience.[36]

However, by the beginning of 1977, the crucial first step had been achieved: a core of the peasantry had been politicized and organized into cells which could now serve as a base. Next came the setting up of a people's militia to counter the frequent armed incursions of the ELF and to tip the balance of power in favour of the majority of the people. All this was felt to be necessary long before the question of land ownership for women could even be touched upon.

At the same time, 1977 saw a string of EPLF victories on the battlefront. In April Afabet was won, the second in a string of seven towns taken by the People's Army between March and August that year. It would now be much easier to tip the balance of power in the area. The landlords no longer had Ethiopian authorities or ELF supporters to turn to. Land – always the central issue in the minds of the oppressed people of the area – began to be openly discussed at mass meetings.

In May 1978 the landlords made a last-ditch attempt to hang on to their power and status. They organized a large demonstration in the hope of rallying people to their side by means of threats. Afabet was packed with slogans such as "Our women are subject to Koranic laws, they shall not attend [EPLF] schools", "May those not joining us beget black dogs" and "May those not joining us be denied access to Heaven". But the era of the landlords was over and eventually the six organizers of the demonstration were exposed by the masses and arrested by the EPLF.

Soon after, the People's Assembly and the Peasants' Association drew up plans for land redistribution and started to implement them in two distinct stages. The first stage involved the land of the landlords. The rich peasants were excluded from this stage in order to prevent any alliances developing between them and the landlords. The land taken away from the landlords was redistributed to tenants and middle and poor peasants, but as the EPLF stresses: "it was not possible to distribute land to women at this stage".

The second stage involved all the land and was far more thorough. By now the People's Assembly and the People's Militia were strongly established and the process of land redistribution took place in an atmosphere of confidence which openly challenged the authority of the landlords. Land was distributed to women in this final stage. It was done according to the policies established by the EPLF (see Appendix 4), under which the rights of women are as follows:

1. In the event of a divorce, the land is divided between the parties equitably.
2. Widows and their children receive full rights to land allocation.
3. A childless woman receives half of a family plot.
4. A woman past the age of marriage (a spinster) receives half of a family plot.
5. A woman past the age of 25 who is unfit for marriage and who may live with her family or relations receives half of a family plot.
6. A woman who comes back to her village upon being divorced, may according to choice receive land in her home or her husband's village.[36]

Wadi Labca demonstrates the important role of People's Assemblies, the representative organizations of people political power. They are the vehicle for pushing forward the class struggle from which Eritrean women are not excluded by being hidden in the household. There can be no doubt that land redistribution has tremendously strengthened the position of women; The enthusiasm generated in them is proof of this, and the reason for it is clear too. As Abrahedsien Girmai told me:

> Land reform is a result of our struggle. Women are fighting at the front, we too are fighting here and as a result we gain equal rights. In our village, the EPLF land-reform programme has redistributed land and given it even to women without husbands. If a woman does not have children she takes half the plot. If she does she takes the same amount as a man. If a woman is rich she gets someone to work with her and pays him. Otherwise she gets someone to plough for her (see page 53) and gives him a share of the harvest; or the village collectively helps her while she makes coffee, *injeera* and so on in return. Every woman owns land either individually or with men. And women take part in agriculture a lot more. I myself till the land and do some harvesting for others; in return they plough for me.

If the "new equitable base" which the EPLF was aiming to create has already been achieved in some areas, the next question is: how will production be organized? So far, by democratizing land ownership (rather than nationalizing large chunks of land) the EPLF has shown a consciousness of the dialectical relationship between the development of productive forces and class struggle. The same issues now arise in another form over the question of the organization of production. Unlike in Mozambique where hastily created collective farms soon had to be abandoned as failures, the EPLF has taken a careful and realistic line. In the National Democratic Programme of 1977 it aimed to: "make big nationalised farms and extensive farms requiring modern techniques state-farms and use their produce for the benefit of the masses"; and "abolish feudal land relations . . . and strive to introduce cooperative farms by creating conditions of cooperation and mutual assistance so as to develop a modern and advanced system of agriculture and animal husbandry".[37] By 1984 this had been altered to: "convert big farms requiring modern techniques into state farms and use their produce for the benefit of the people";

"implement an equitable distribution of land to make the land benefit the tiller"; and "encourage the peasants to adopt modern agricultural techniques"[37] (see Appendix 1). As an agricultural officer at Nacfa explained to me in 1988: "We have found that in very large units like big collective farms people lose their initiative and motivation. We do have farms run locally in a co-operative way and of course we have household production".

Household production poses its own problems, however. As China's "economic reforms" of 1978 have shown, household production (there called "rural responsibility system") does increase agricultural output but is accompanied by the development of serious inequalities between households and a major deterioration in the position of women. Women in rural China now face a situation where their labour is under the supervision of the head of the household (rather than the collective), pushing them back under under familial authority. At the same time products of their labour are controlled by a rural economy whose management structure is in the hands of men.[38]

There are obvious differences between Eritrea today and China in 1978 and there is no doubt that the EPLF needs to prioritize food production, but will it be at the expense of women's emancipation? The answer to this is related to a number of other issues. The small size of individual plots is likely to limit output after a certain stage in technological development since mechanization is particularly subject to economies of scale. In addition, the highly publicized view that the ideal agricultural unit for Third World countries is the small family farm, in which more labour will be applied per acre than in any other system, disguises the fact that this intensity of labour is demanded by the continuous threat of economic disaster and inevitably involves the extreme exploitation of family members. Thus the EPLF's stated aims of equitable land distribution and encouraging the adoption of modern agricultural technology seem likely to promote the formation of co-operatives. The degree of co-operativization in marketing, shared labour or complete merger of holdings will depend as much on political as on economic goals.

7 Marriage

Land reform is a means of transforming the economic base of feudal- and clan-based society, but the ideologies of such a society are extremely tenacious. They persist long after the base is removed[39] and continue to play a major role in determining the position of women. As a result, for example, urban families reproduce the same relationships of oppression which have been handed down to them by their rural landowning ancestors and which still persist in the villages. Since these ideologies and relationships are generated and regenerated within the patriarchal extended family, the basic unit of feudal and clan society, it is the family itself which must be dismantled and transformed. In order to perform this extremely complex and sensitive task, the Eritrean People's Liberation Front (EPLF) decided to tackle the heart of the family: marriage, the chief determinant of a woman's life.

As we have seen, Eritrea is a society with a variety of social formations, ranging from communal and animist through clan society to various stages in the development of feudalism. These are influenced by trade with capitalist markets outside, and by the effects of colonialism.

Marriage in such a society is defined by a multitude of varying customary laws, and describing these in all their complexity is beyond the scope of this book. Instead we will look at certain essential principles of marriage in a peasant society in a very different part of the world, in India. There, as in Eritrea, the basic unit is the patriarchal extended family, but colonial capitalism has interacted with the social formations of advanced feudalism. We will see how far the principles of marriage in such a society also serve as guidelines to "traditional" marriage in different communities in Eritrea.

The first and most essential of these principles – the logical reason for all the others – is that marriage must consolidate the patriarchal line and family property. As such it must be an alliance between two families rather than two individuals. The second principle – a direct result of the patrilineal structure – is that marriage must produce sons. The third is that marriage must serve to control female sexual activities (since illegitimate children are a threat to the patrilineal family and property) and provide an arena where the fear of women's sexuality is generated and regenerated. Finally, marriage is a means of handing control of all these arrangements for propagation of the family to the older male members of the family.

In Eritrea all the women I spoke to with the exception of Kunamas who do not have a patriarchal and patrilineal family structure, told me that not only was preserving the family line important but that, as in India, it was the single most important factor in marriage arrangements. It was so crucial that the eligibility of a girl for marriage was assessed on this basis. Women from different ethnic groups – Tigre, Tigrinya and Billen – and Orthodox Christians, Protestants, Catholics and Muslims told me that "purity of blood" was the most important consideration. Next came "wealth" and "beauty" in that order. But what is "blood purity"? Sembatu Bakheet, meticulous as ever, explained it quite clearly:

> When a girl gets married, of course she must come from the same community and religion. After that the most important consideration is her blood. Her family should have no connection with slaves[34] or with Hamiens[40] (minstrels). She should not practise witchcraft and should have no leprosy. After these come the importance of wealth and beauty.

Preserving the family line is followed closely by a drive to consolidate family property, so it is not by chance that "wealth" is an important qualification. As in India, alliances with well-off landowning families and the exchange of property through large dowries and bride prices is the dream of those who arrange marriages. As Sara Indrias put it: "the boy's family look for land and economic position – animals, houses and money – when arranging a marriage; the girl is less important".

In Eritrea as in India, marriage arrangements involve two separate types of expenditure. First there is the wedding itself. Here, lavish celebrations are dependent on the production of a reasonable surplus and therefore are more characteristic of well-off communities. It is what every family aspires to, however, because the pressure to be lavish is characteristic of feudal societies, linked to conspicuous consumption and a display of wealth. The wedding described to me by Akiar Hajaji, from the aristocratic group among the Habab of Sahel, was very similar to that of couples from similar nomadic groups in India. There too a large amount of food is prepared (six goats were slaughtered at Akiar's wedding), the groom can bring any number of guests to the feast, and the women eat separately.

Second there is the giving of dowries (paid by the bride's family) or bride prices (paid by the groom's family). In general Muslims pay bride prices, and Christians in Eritrea and Hindus in India pay dowries, although in each case there are exceptions. These payments are duties on the part of the family whose purpose is to strengthen the clan. But they occur in a society constantly subjected to external forces and internal upheavals. For example, the lowlands of Eritrea were never totally isolated from the outside world. In the early nineteenth century, butter produced here was taken to Massawa to be sold in Saudi Arabia. Later, as a result of Italian colonialism, better medical and veterinary facilities became available to the pastoralist "serfs" and it has been argued that this led to new class formation.

Women like Akiar described to me the effects of these changes, and how the rules of marriage-arranging and the associated oppressive relationships remained the same while bride prices rose steeply. The increase in bride prices caused differentials, pauperization and migration to towns, which in turn created new classes. All these processes deeply intensified the oppression of women, colonialism offering them none of the advantages of capitalism but at the same time denying them the few obligatory safeguards of feudal society. She told me:

> "My father is a farmer, my mother a housewife. They had a big plot and six pairs of oxen to plough. Nine years ago they arranged my marriage without consulting me. My husband is also from the same tribe. For bride price my husband gave me 3 special outfits, 2 pairs of gold earrings, 1 nosering, 15 grams of gold, clothes for my parents, 2 quintals of grain, 300 Ethiopian dollars and 5 cows. . . . This was the average bride price although bride prices had been rising for quite a long time. . . . These high bride prices created many problems. They placed people under pressure to pay them and some people sold their houses and animals just to pay or went into debt and ended up becoming very poor. Others failed to pay and this resulted in disgrace. Poor men had to save for years in order to marry. Many girls had to become second or third wives of rich men, or else could not marry at all and had to migrate to towns and become prostitutes or domestic servants."

Eritrea is not only a society which has been in flux during the last 50 years; it is a society with a variety of modes of production which have been in a fairly intense state of interaction during the last 200 years. Here, unlike in India or Ethiopia which had fully fledged feudal societies, feudalism had only just begun to emerge before capitalist influences appeared. As a result feudal institutions do not exist, and feudal classes with specific roles in production are found only in certain limited areas. Similarly, the rules which determine women's position, although extremely oppressive, are also less rigid. For example, women are expected to be virgins at marriage and can be sent home in disgrace if they are not, or even if they do not happen to bleed during first intercourse. Yet some women do have pre-marital sex and there are customs in certain groups which institutionalize methods to deal with this contingency and preserve the marriage[42] Similarly, while pre-marital and extra-marital sex is strictly forbidden for women, many women told me that they it was not uncommon for men to have relationships, sometimes regular ones, with women they did not officially marry. Again, while remarriage is said to be very difficult for women, one does come across a significant proportion of women who have remarried (although usually on payment of a large dowry). Eritrean society's state of flux, and the interactions between different groups, are also reflected in marriage payments. Among Billens from the vicinity of Karen, for example, both the bride's father and the groom's father make payments. Gaddam and Maharite related these customs back to the origins of their group:

> In the nineteenth century Agos from Ethiopia came to the Billen area. They had no religion [they were animists] but the people in the Billen area were Muslim pastoralists. The two groups merged, the Agos taught [the Muslims] settled agriculture and themselves became Muslims. Later, Catholic missionaries came and converted about half of us to Christianity. Now in Billen villages, the older people would probably be Muslim and the younger generation would be Christians. We pay bride price during engagement. The father of the groom, if he is rich, says: "I'll give 12 cows to the bride, 6 of the cows in cash and 6 animals." There is a year of engagement . . . and during this year the groom's family visits the bride's family with gifts, including animals, whenever there is a special occasion – when a birth is celebrated, for example. On the wedding day all these extra gifts are taken into account and the bride's father gives something to the groom's father.

With the propagation of the patriarchal line and the strengthening of patriarchal property clearly established as the main purpose of marriage, the second principle – the need to produce sons – automatically follows on. All the women whom I asked about Eritrean traditional society confirmed that having sons was crucially important. If a woman did not produce sons, and particularly if she was unable to have any children, it was accepted that her husband would marry again. As in any Third World country where a large proportion of children die because of poor health conditions, this compulsion to have sons – and sons who survive – relegates a woman to an endless cycle of pregnancy and childbirth. The only ethnic group where this is not the case are the Kunamas. Here, as Zainab Ibrahim, a Muslim from Barentu[43] told me: "we prefer the first child to be a boy to help on the farm but in general we prefer girls".

Although the patriarchal family demands that children be produced, a woman's sexual desires and needs are still a matter closer to the devil than real life.[44] Eritrean society takes the third aspect of marriage, the generation and regeneration of fear of women's sexuality, as a matter of extreme importance. This attitude is not only a product of patriarchal peasant society; the idea of woman as an evil temptress is inherent in both Christianity and Islam. (Again the Kunamas are an exception, even Muslim Kunamas: they see female sexuality as something positive.) A wide range of customs and attitudes is created by this ideology, encompassing clitorodectomy which is supposed to restrict female desire, the veiling and segregation of women, stories of witches and she-devils, and much else. Behind it, however, is the recognition that free sexual activity on the part of women could lead to "illegitimate" children who would undermine the patriarchal line, challenge patriarchal laws of inheritance and in this way threaten partriarchal property.

In accordance with these fears, a girl is taught from early childhood "to be shy", not to look at or speak to men, and, as she grows older, not even to speak when men are around. She is taught to be withdrawn, restrained, obedient and passive. Her mother is given the responsibility of keeping her in line. As Elsa told me, "If a girl is very lively there are comments such as 'she is too sexy', 'her mother has not brought her up properly', and 'she has not been circumcised'. Since girls are often very close to their mothers it makes it even harder for them to rebel because then their mothers would be blamed."

In Eritrea, circumcision is the ultimate expression of society's fear of female sexuality. It is practised in two forms: clitoridectomy, the excision of the clitoris, is common in both the highlands and lowlands; and infibulation, the removal and suturing of the labia, is particularly widespread among Muslims in the lowlands. Female circumcision is rare among Kunamas, except in those groups among them who are Muslims – in other words those influenced by the ideology of neighbouring semi-feudal groups. Infibulation is the more dangerous practice.

It can lead not only to heavy bleeding, infection, urine retention and tetanus but to haemorrhage and death during childbirth. It also means that sexual intercourse for the first time is a painful and traumatic experience with the tearing apart of the labia.

Infibulation obviously deters a woman from pre-marital sexual activity but it cannot affect female sexual desire as it is claimed to do, since the sites of sexual desire are all over the body and cannot be excised. This point is emphasised by Dr Nerayo Tekle Michael, director of the EPLF's Public Health Programme. However, it has a powerful psychological effect, making women feel that their own sexuality is something undesirable. Proverbs and saying reinforce this. For example: "A vagina without infibulation is ugly, it is like a house without a door."

Male sexual desire, while also seen as dangerous, is at least considered "natural". It is regarded as a response to the "temptation" posed by a woman's body and even her face, and so it is thought best for women to be veiled and segregated. The degree to which this occurs varies from community to community, ranging from a long scarf covering only the hair and part of the face, to almost complete segregation. On the whole, veils and segregation are commoner among Muslims but the most extreme form I was told about was among the Catholic Billens. Maharite Tekhle, from Ajerbub, described it to me:

> In our nationality women traditionally do not work outside the house. They grind the flour, look after the children and only after sunset go out to look after the calves. . . . Up to the age of 10 children play together. Then the boy goes with his father, the girl with her mother. Among Billen, men do not know what their wives look like. When the man comes home, the wife goes and hides in a dark room. She passes him his food and other things he needs from there. She sees him but he can't see her.

At the same time Billen culture has its own stabilizing and pacificatory elements the occasional licence which maintains the everyday restrictions. Maharite told me:

There is a ceremony called *Hebo* which takes place after a death in the family. The closest female relatives of a woman come and dance. They dance shaking their heads. The men come and watch. They make comments: "She's pretty" or "She's ugly!" Once a man in our village saw a woman whom he thought was very beautiful. He said to a friend: "Please introduce me to that woman." Actually she was his wife and he did not know. Later he went home and said to her: "Why don't you ever join the dance?"

Finally, interdependent on the need for male labour and out of the fear of female sexuality comes the last major principle of arranged marriage in much of India: the total decision-making power it gives to the older males of the family. In Eritrea this power is traditionally handed to one man. As a Tigrinya woman describing her own family explained, the reason is that one man controls the land:

> All my father's family lived in the same village and shared the same land. My father and my uncles ploughed together and we always passed feast days in my grandfather's house. I never called my uncles "uncle" – they were like fathers to me. I couldn't separate them from my own father, just as you couldn't separate who owned what in the family.

While control of land gives the patriarch authority, control of labour determines his role. This particular division of power serves to control the sexual activities of younger members of the family, particularly males, channelling their energies into productive labour. The control is reinforced by the notion that work is inherently more worthy than sexual activity, and that sex is "dirty". As feudalism develops further (beyond the stage it reached in Eritrea), both the concept of decadence and decadence itself are encouraged since rich men are able to make sexual activity with women of a lower class a part of conspicuous consumption.

It is striking that in the patriarchal extended family, in Eritrea, older women have on the face of it no role in arranging marriages. Here too the communal society of the Kunamas provides an opposite. As Zainab Ibrahim explained:

> We have two ways of arranging marriage. In one the mother builds a house for her daughter and invites young men who are her friends. The girl chooses one from among them. In the second type of arrangement the mother of the boy goes with gifts to the mother of the girl who gives them to her daughter. If she wants to get married she accepts the gifts, otherwise she returns them – that is how my marriage was arranged.

Like marriage payments, the hierarchy of age also is influenced by external factors. In this case they have weakened it, although they have not necessarily improved the position of women. Industrialization, migration to the towns, and women's wage labour and access to cash have brought changes. For example, middle-class women in towns now belong to *ukubs* or savings clubs which they use to contribute to their daughters' dowry payments, and this means they have more of a voice in marriage arrangements. Similarly, if a nuclear unit of the extended family migrates to a town the parents are more likely to arrange their own daughter's marriage, in consultation with older members of the extended family who still reside in the countryside. This is what happened in Davit Hailemariam's account (see page 27), but as we have seen it did not make life easier for the bride.

These are some of the major aspects of marriage in Eritrea's patriarchal peasant communities; there are many others. Each of them contributes to the comprehensive control which society holds over women's lives. Together these factors create the greatest oppression of all – self-imposed withdrawal and passivity, which goes deep into the consciousness of many women. This is not because, as is sometimes thought in the West, these women are unaware of their oppression. On the contrary, it is precisely because they are aware of it that the majority feel that withdrawal and passivity are the only means of self-preservation. The minority who think and act otherwise are the rebels.

While Eritrean society is not essentially very different from many other patriarchal peasant societies in South Asia or Africa, the way the EPLF has tackled the subject of women's oppression is different from any other revolutionary movement. In Africa and South Asia, too often the approach has been: "we must not offend the masses so we cannot tamper with traditional culture at this stage" or else when there is a question of supporting a woman who rebels: "we would like to support her but by doing so we will alienate the community and get a bad reputation ourselves."

The EPLF on the other hand has made it a systematic part of its policy. In increasing numbers, girls have been helped to avoid attempts to force them into marriages, by physically removing them where necessary. Experiences like those of Hamida Ahmad Mohamed, a Rashaida woman of 22 whom I met in Heshkep, are far from extraordinary:

> I am from Kassala. My father is a merchant; he went to live in Saudi Arabia ten years ago. In February last year [in 1988] I was married to a very old man – older than 60. It was done because my father wanted to marry the man's young daughter in exchange. After seven days of my marriage I became very ill, maybe for psychological reasons. My uncle took me to the medical centre run by the EPLF and after three months there I decided to join the EPLF. I had recovered and I came to the field. I sent my relatives a letter from here. The old man was very angry and refused to let my father marry his daughter. My father was angry too at first, but a relative wrote to him and told him that I had become a fighter and that I was OK and he could visit me. And recently he came here and saw that I really was alright.

The EPLF has undertaken the reform of traditional marriage laws, carrying it out in the same systematic and carefully planned manner as land reform and the establishment of people's political power, by first studying the situation, then creating the necessary pre-conditions, and finally embarking on detailed discussions which enable the masses themselves to change the law.

Before we look at these processes let us look at the people who were to set them in motion, the EPLF members themselves, and their own attitudes to marriage and sexual relations. As revolutionaries they had left their homes, their parents, their property and their pasts very far behind and entered an intense new arena. There, as a fighter from the front line whom I met in Orota told me:

> The memories of my childhood are like memories from another world. If someone who knew me reminds me: "You used to like this" or "you used to do that" then of course I remember. But I don't think about it much. I am not in close touch with my family. And although I love them, I don't miss them. Because here I have found a deeper, more complete love and support.

Thus in the EPLF a new identity – an all-embracing dedication to the struggle – erased all the other identities of family, region, clan and class. Despite this, however, the attitudes to sex and sexuality created by tradition remained deep in people's consciousness. In recognition of this the EPLF thought it necessary that their members learn a new sexual morality. But what was the sexual morality to be? In the first eight years when it was essentially only a fighting force, EPLF cadres were expected quite simply to be celibate.

Celibacy of course also meant asexuality. How was this put into practice? As Trish Silkin writes:

> Men and women recruits underwent separate military training and were expected to have learnt a new asexual body language by the time they had graduated from the training school and joined mixed units. Female fighters were given baggy trousers and loose shirts to wear, which concealed their figures, and they were required to keep their shirt buttoned up to the neck.[41]

In other words, the idea of female sexuality being a dangerous temptation was retained from traditional culture. Male fighters were taught to subdue a sexual urge which was nevertheless considered "natural". As a male fighter told Silkin:

> It is not that I don't have any sexual feelings but I have to repress [them] because I know that my male chauvinism will come out in my sexual relations with women. Usually the man takes the initiative in these things, not because it is inherent in us but because of our dominant position in society. Any woman comrade has to trust me, to work side by side with me confidently, and for that she needs to know that I think of her as a comrade and not just as a woman. You know that if you initiate sexual relations with a woman, you are disgracing the front and betraying your comrades.[41]

The fighters also learned a collective responsibility for enforcing celibacy:

> If a comrade failed and the issue came to a meeting, I remember how embarrassed I used to feel. You also know how embarrassed they feel because they have failed their comrades. So, if a man and a woman start to be seen going off alone together you start questioning it. You ask what kind of relationship it is, whether it is a good relationship or whether something is up. You keep an eye on them and if you realize it is more than a normal friendship you question them. "Is your relationship a clean one or is it something else?" And if it is more you tell them that you like people to have close relationships but it's against our norms to have that kind of a relationship. So you bring it to their attention privately. That's what you're supposed to do. If there is no change you bring it to the attention of your comrades.[41]

Here we see some of the attitudes of traditional society: that sex is not clean, for example; but compounded by the fact that having a sexual relationship is letting the comrades down and is therefore a matter of shame.

Thus at this stage, there was a recognition that traditional sexual relationships were too closely associated with oppressive gender and social relationships, and so they had to be rejected. But as yet nothing had replaced them, and sex remained taboo. In 1977, however, at about the same time that the first land reforms were being carried out, the EPLF policy on marriage and sexual relationships was changed. As Ande Michael Kahsai explained:

At the 1977 Organisational Congress thousands of letters were received asking when the marriage law would be promulgated. By then there were a large number of women in the EPLF and many of the EPLF members were young people . . . also we were no longer only a fighting force. . . . In the early days marriage was not an issue – we were always on the move. We would spend the day in one place and move to another to sleep. We would eat with our belts on ready for action. It was not possible to think of marriage or sex, but later when things changed, the question imposed itself. The same year the new marriage law was promulgated. It was to apply immediately to EPLF members and in time was to replace the customary law codes which regulated marriage in the liberated zones.

The new marriage law banned "feudal marriage customs [specifically child betrothal, polygyny, and concubinage] which are based on the supremacy of men over women, arbitrary and coercive arrangements and which do not safeguard the welfare of children". It was "based on the free choice of both parties, monogamy, the equal rights of both sexes and legal guarantees of the interests of women and children". In form and content the law is almost identical to the 1950 Marriage Law of the Chinese People's Republic. It was not followed by a flood of marriage applications, however. Some cadres held back because they felt that by being too eager they might raise suspicions about their earlier conduct. Others continued to feel, because of the earlier system, that marriage was a diversion from the struggle for Eritrean independence. After this initial period, though, the number of applications did increase and by the mid-1980s more than 1,500 marriages had taken place.

After 1977 marriage became a common topic of discussion among the fighters. In 1980 the Department of Political Education and Culture held a seminar for fighters in which the old system of marriage was examined,[41] the principles of the new system were explained, and participants were asked to comment on those issues which concerned them (see Appendix 6b). One of the main topics of discussion was pre-marital sex. It was opposed by some people, mainly men, young and old.

However, this view was countered by both women and men with arguments that women's traditional sexual passivity is not biological but based on their subordinate social role, and that the female sexual urge is not only equal to but sometimes stronger than that of men.

After the seminar such discussions were held regularly, and some of the issues involved were incorporated into a questionnaire which couples have to fill in when they want to marry. Topics include the difference between love and infatuation, the need to get to know each other well enough, the need to have pre-marital sex and the importance of privacy. As a fighter commented in 1986:

> The important thing is: how compatible are you? You are not going to be a hundred per cent compatible in everything so you have to find out where to compromise. And that take time. That is the best thing the Front has done – giving people the chance to go together for two or three years before they marry or decide not to marry. People have privacy and you have the chance to discuss many things and to decide whether you get on or not.[41]

Since 1982, living arrangements have been modified to allow couples more privacy:

> Before 1982 up to ten people lived and slept together so it was difficult to have any kind of a relationship. Now we have built houses which are just big enough for one or two people that we call "you and me" houses or "soviets". Not only can we have a girlfriend officially, but these houses allow us privacy to pursue our relationship. This solved the problem of people getting married just for the sake of being alone with their partner.[41]

Traces of the old attitudes do remain, attitudes which, incidentally, are also present in left-wing political circles in Britain and America. In the EPLF, for example, women and men are said to be still inhibited about women taking the sexual initiative, although they are encouraged to do so. Women are also extremely cautious about starting sexual relationships because they feel worried about the possibility of a relationship breaking up. According to Trish Silkin:

a number of women reported that they had turned down requests to start relationships because they did not feel that they had sufficient in common with the men concerned for the relationships to last. It is generally acknowledged that women are more vulnerable than men when relationships end. The main reason for this is that while women are no longer expected to be virgins when they marry, both men and women feel more comfortable if a woman loses her virginity to the man she eventually marries. To combat this the EPLF encourages its members to have "open" relationships and all marriage applicants are asked whether relationships were open or hidden: of the couples in my sample, ten had an open relationship before they were married although in most cases they were hidden at the beginning, in one case for as much as 18 months.[41]

EPLF members started the struggle to reorganize marriage in the liberated zone from 1977 onwards. As in the case of the establishment of people's assemblies and land reform, the areas where the customary marriage laws could be changed were those totally under EPLF control. However, an area initially under full EPLF control might become a contested area with Ethiopian troops present. In this case the reformed law might become difficult to use in practice and might even be temporarily abandoned.[45]

The process of reform has essentially been one of discussion. When the people were convinced that changes were needed, they were involved in making them. This is why the first stage of each reformed law was specific to a given area, and often different in detail from that reformed law in other areas, although all of them fell within the broad principles laid down by the EPLF. They are now being brought into line and standardized for the whole country. The steps involved in implementing this transformation were similar to those for land reform. First there was an in-depth study of the situation and the forces for and against change. Second, essential preconditions were established, obtaining the support of religious leaders. Third, change was gradually implemented step by step.

Sembatu Bakheet, herself involved as an EPLF cadre, explained the process which occurred in mid-eastern Eritrea:

Marriage   137

> First the EPLF cadres and the representatives of the People's Assembly had a meeting and discussed the customary laws of Muslims and Christians; they chose the most important ones. They fixed [the minimum] marriage age at 17, and decided to prohibit forced marriage and infibulation. [They] allowed divorce by women, [and] laid down a maximum for the amount of gold given at weddings and the amount food prepared. They came to agreement on these changes. Then they had a bigger meeting with EPLF cadres, People's Assembly and religious leaders – Muslim, Protestant, Catholic and Orthodox. They agreed on all these points. For infibulation they passed the law, and for clitorodectomy they passed a law saying that the family had to report to the People's Assembly who would ensure that there was no infibulation performed at the same time as the clitoridectomy. Then the laws were read to the people. There was some opposition from them but since the religious leaders supported the laws, the opposition was easily overcome.

I asked Sembatu how the support of the religious leaders was obtained:

> It took several years of discussions by the cadres before these meetings were held. It was not new to the religious leaders – they had been convinced by this time. It took ten years in mid-eastern Eritrea. But after that the meetings between EPLF cadres and the People's Assembly took a week, and the cadres, the People's Assembly and religious leaders took only a day.

These experiences show the crucial importance of sensitivity to both traditional culture and the correct pace of change. In view of this, all reformed laws make provision for gradual change, for example by allowing parents to arrange a marriage with the consent of the bride and groom. The discussions occurring in the process of reform reveal the persistent preoccupation with female sexuality. Despite this[41] a bride's virginity has ceased to be a reason for annulling the marriage in the highland laws, and the bride's future parents-in-law are prohibited from having her virginity attested before the wedding night. In the region north of Asmara strict penalties have been imposed for infringing this: a man may be fined as much as 700 Ethiopian dollars or serve a commensurate term of imprisonment for attempting to send back his bride because she is not a virgin.

Meanwhile in mid-eastern Eritrea, discussion centred round whether female circumcision should be forbidden by the marriage laws. Religious leaders, as Sembatu related, supported a ban, on the grounds that infibulation damaged women's health. However, EPLF cadres decided not to take the legislation further and extend the ban to clitoridectomy because "this would take the argument beyond women's health and into the sphere of women's rights to and capacity for sexual pleasure which would alienate the people from the more moderate reform".[41]

Will clitoridectomy also be banned in the future? The structures exist for this to happen, but as with the subject of marriage, "the question must impose itself". Undoubtedly it will, as traditional semi-feudal culture is gradually transformed into modern socialist culture in Eritrea.

8 Health

For many people, the thought of medical services in a Third World country conjures up stereotypical images of that colonial trio – poverty, ignorance and disease. They visualize them being dealt with by another picture-book character, the dedicated aid and charity worker who struggles out of the goodness of his or her heart to save the lives of these anonymous victims. Eritrea shatters these myths. Here the images are of crops destroyed by Ethiopian soldiers, towns flattened to rubble, young people permanently disabled, children emaciated by famine because food is not allowed to reach them, babies with terrible injuries and burns, young Eritrean women doctors in mobile units at the battlefront, traditional midwives with modern kits, and miles of camouflaged hospital buildings where the most complex operations are being performed. These images force one to face reality: the main and overwhelming cause of illness, injury and pain here is the long and inherently genocidal war. Health and medical services, if they are to be effective, must be a systematic part of the process of development for and by the people.

Eritrea's health problems are acute and horrifying. They can be divided into two categories: those caused directly by the war; and those which are the result of social formations and natural factors such as famine and drought, exacerbated by the war. In real life the two categories are not separable. The families who are bombed and burnt with napalm are the same ones whose land has been eaten into by colonialism, whose children suffer from malnutrition, and whose young daughters-in-law risk death in frequent childbirth. Dr Nerayo Tekle Michael, co-ordinator of the Eritrean Public Health Programme, summed up the nature of problems simply and poignantly:

> An old woman with a severely emaciated child in her arms recently came to see me and asked despairingly, "What shall we do with this child? His mother died a month after giving birth. His father is unable to care for him – he himself suffers from TB. I am the child's grandmother but I have nothing for him." What shall we do with this child, with that pregnant woman, the young, the old? These are questions health workers in rural Eritrea face daily. They are difficult questions when the needs are so widespread and the resources so limited.[46]

The answers to these questions tell of a struggle lasting nearly twenty years, with its ups and downs, its setbacks and victories, in the course of which some important basic strategies have been developed. These strategies would be useful to any Third World country in crisis. First, all good aspects of traditional services must be preserved and built upon, and bad ones must be rejected wholeheartedly. Second, services must be for the people as a whole and not for a small elite. (The implications of this are enormous: for example, preventative medicine and public health must take precedence over specialist medicine; primary health care and the health of women of childbearing age must be a focus of attention; and available resources should go to health clinics in preference to expensive hospitals.) Third, the people themselves must participate in almost the entire process of health care. Finally, health improvement must be part of a holistic approach to development, linked closely to the provision of basic resources like drinking water, a concern for the environment, the emancipation of women and much else.

In this field as in so many others, the Eritrean People's Liberation Front (EPLF) had to start from scratch. In 1970 when it was formed there were hospitals in towns such as Asmara and Decamare but there were no established medical services at all in rural Eritrea. In the countryside, traditional healers were called in to the sick and dying. These highly respected members of the community still provide much of the treatment available in rural Eritrea. They use a variety of methods, ranging from blood-letting and exorcism to traditional herbal therapeutics. According to the Eritrean Public Health Programme (EPHP), these methods are on the whole probably beneficial to society but do include some practices which are overtly harmful.

Between 1970 and 1974 no systematic services could be set up. The only medical staff were a few "barefoot" doctors, people with basic medical and first-aid skills, and a few highly skilled medical workers operating in mobile units. During the next two years, however, with a fresh influx of people including medical workers from urban areas, the EPLF was able to establish two hospitals to provide basic treatment, and also several mobile and stationary clinics. From 1976 to 1978, with the civil war virtually over and the EPLF making considerable military gains, medical services were set up in the towns under EPLF control and a comprehensive urban and rural health scheme was established. In 1978 – when the strategic withdrawal took place the EPLF carried out one of its characteristic operations, astonishing in both conception and implementation. Urban hospitals in towns like Karen were dismantled and relocated in the rural lowlands. This was when the Central Hospital in Orota was established – more precisely during the Ethiopian sixth offensive.

In the period 1979 to 1982 there was a major expansion of health services and two new programmes were set in motion. The Eritrean Public Health Programme focused on public health in the liberated zone, particularly in the context of massive displaced populations. The Eritrean Medical Association took on the task of restructuring the health services and expanding primary health care in the rural areas, with the aim of developing a nationwide system of rural health care by the end of 1990.

As Nerayo Tekle Michael states:

> We have a plan which will help us move closer towards the achievement of a dream. We have our capabilities, the basic ingredients of success. These include a smoothly functioning administrative infrastructure inside the country; the availability

of manpower ready and able to be trained and to train; a high degree of community participation; and, above all, an official total commitment to this, our second struggle for liberation.[46]

Underlying the plan and pushing it forward are two separate but constantly interlinking themes. The first aims to meet the needs of the present: to deal with the horrific injuries of the fighters and the civilian population attacked by the Ethiopians, and to help victims of drought and famine. The second theme aims to build a secure and self-reliant future which will enable the Eritrean people to fulfil their true potential in terms of production, dynamism and creativity. Both themes have to be executed simultaneously: one cannot wait for the other; in Eritrea there is no "after the revolution . . ." This is reflected in the approach, attitudes and expectations of the people in every health centre, clinic and hospital.

Orota Central Hospital is a remarkable place. I stayed there for about a fortnight along with many other foreign guests on my first trip to Eritrea. I remember getting down from the landrover at the threshold of the hospital after the ten-hour overnight trip from Port Sudan. I had heard about the base at Orota and wondered where it was – this was my first experience of the liberated zone. Then I was shown some stone steps and I clambered down them. I remember the first sharp cock-crow of morning as I entered the 6-km-long building in the shadow of tall mountains; it was so well camouflaged that I had missed it altogether.

In the next few evenings and nights I was taken round the hospital and its associated complexes. I saw major operations including brain surgery which are normally associated with hospitals in the West, being carried out successfully under conditions which are achievable in any Third World country. I looked round maternity units and dental surgeries constructed out of large containers, and visited pharmaceutical laboratories where, in a step towards self-reliance, essential drugs and intravenous fluids were being formulated from imported raw materials.[47] I talked to people receiving treatment, and to doctors, surgeons and health workers – most of them women.

Their experiences demonstrated to me how health work is part of social change, part of development and an integral part of the armed struggle.

Asmeret, who had once been a clandestine worker in Asmara, was now working in the pharmacy. She told me how she came to the field, and about her experiences as a health worker at the front lines:

> One day in Asmara, the enemy got to know that my sisters and I were involved with the EPLF. They came to our house and they took my three sisters. The youngest was only 13, they took her too. I was 18 at the time. I escaped through a back window. I waited till they destroyed our house. Then I escaped. I went to my comrades and they brought me to the field. I was taken to Sahel and there I had my military training. After that they assigned me for medical training. I worked at the central hospital at Sakerkate, two days' journey east of Orota – at that time it was the biggest hospital. There were a lot of wounded fighters. We learnt how to dress wounds and how to take care of patients. I was trained three months for medical and three for surgical and then assigned to surgical. I worked for a year and took a course for operation technicians. I learnt how to give infusions, and to diagnose and perform operations like amputations and foreign body removal. In this training, the doctor supports you but you do everything yourself.
>
> I stayed on in that hospital for some years and then was sent to Karen as a barefoot doctor and OR [oral rehydration] technician. This was in 1978, when we were withdrawing from Karen. I worked in different hospitals. Then I was assigned to work in mobile teams in Barka and Senhit. There are about twenty members in each team; I was OR technician and anaesthetist, moving in the front line doing urgent surgery and sending patients back to main hospitals. We did not have many anaesthetists – we had to work 24 hours a day for a week at a time. We would be ready and we would follow an offensive. The Ethiopians were using heavy artillery and when they retreated they would bomb and burn the civilian population with napalm. Children, pregnant women [and] old people were dying and we were struggling to save their lives. For five years I

was with mobile teams; then after Tessenei was captured in 1984 I came here to work in OR for a year. Since then I have been training to be a pharmacy technician.

Just as people can switch from one speciality to another according to the need of the hour, there is also in Eritrea no hierarchy in the health services, no "doctors and nurses" situation. The workers, many of them very highly skilled, are typically modest. Linesh Gebre Huvet, a small delicate woman who was head of the dental and maxillofacial unit, explained to me that plastic surgery, although it involves a major operation, is not that different from cutting and sewing. "Because that is really what we do," she said, drawing a finger down from her temples to her jawbone, "we have to cut very carefully."

She told me about the unit, and about the people it treated and their attitudes.

In 1979 when this unit was founded, because of lack of experience and shortage of medical supplies we were confined to very minor operations like wound-dressing, treatment of simple fractures and so on. Now, as a result of painfully accumulated experience we are able to perform major surgery including, bone-grafting and plastic surgery.

If we lack the needed equipment we use orthopaedic equipment which we receive from humanitarian organizations, or we sometimes capture it from the enemy – like this dental chair and dental drill, we got them from Karen. From Barentu we got these forceps – small things but very important. . . . We get some "cold" cases like cancer of the jaw and various mouth diseases, but most of our cases are people wounded by shrapnel, bullets and so on. Most of them are fighters but there are civilians too with severe facial deformity caused by bombing. Any facial deformity does have a psychological effect – we see the distress it causes among civilians. But . . . our fighters are different – they don't care about external appearances. Maybe it is because they are accepted by society and because they have dedicated their lives to the struggle, that external deformity does not cause any psychological problem.

Orota Central Hospital is where some of the most complex surgery in the liberated zone takes place, but it serves also as a central reference point. Primary health care and maternal health care are provided by a network of rural health stations which link up to a health centre. It in turn links to the regional hospital, which links to the central hospital. These stations, centres and mobile teams form the backbone of the Eritrean health services.

In May 1989 I was able to visit the Rora mountains, a highland area which stands alone in the middle of lowlands. I saw the Rora Health Centre which was established in 1982, and the five health stations which link up to it. The health station has only one EPLF member – a "barefoot doctor" five village health workers who are trained by staff from Orota Central Hospital; and a trained traditional birth attendant. The village health workers are helped in their tasks by a health committee constituted by the People's Assembly. The most common illnesses are: malnutrition and anaemia; malaria which exacerbates anaemia; tonsilitis; and the common cold. When the health stations cannot cope they refer patients to the health centre, which in turn refers them on if necessary to the regional and central hospitals. When I visited the Rora Health Centre it was clean and had a number of basic drugs: multivitamins, antibiotics, sulpha drugs and anti-malarial preparations. These, the workers told me, were supplied every month from the Orota pharmacy where they were manufactured. The centre was also equipped with the plastic microscope which astonishingly was developed and manufactured by the EPHP, and which, according to an evaluation in 1986, is just as useful as the conventional bench microscope for detecting ova and bacilli.[48] Before most examinations are performed, the patient is given basic health education: for example, on how to deal with respiratory problems and how to prevent trachoma.

In Rora, as elsewhere in Eritrea, the main health problem faced by women is anaemia in pregnancy, exacerbated at times in this area by malaria. The workers told me it is treated by giving a high-protein diet including eggs, which is organized by the health committee. The most severe cases are admitted to the health station, and the rest are sent back to their villages and looked after by the traditional birth attendant. Rora shows what the EPLF is capable of achieving, even in the highly restrictive conditions imposed by the war. Here between 1982–83 and 1986 there has been a 50 per cent reduction in child mortality and a similar reduction in maternal mortality.

Women's lives have been transformed on many different levels simultaneously. Fatma Omer who lives in Bagla village of the Rora district told me about attitudes to infibulation:

> Now people have stopped infibulation. It is bad to be infibulated because a lot of women die while giving birth. I used to be infibulated but I stopped about ten years ago. Before that I had six children and I was restitched each time. Since I stopped I have had four children. [How did she learn about the dangers of infibulation?] I was a member of the EPLF's mass organization – the Women's Union – and when I was pregnant I went to the midwife to give birth. I lost a lot of blood because they had to unstitch my vagina. After the birth the midwife helped me and advised me to stop being infibulated. I accepted her advice . . . no, my husband said nothing about it.

Relationships within the family are also changing: at the health centre a number of fathers had brought their children for treatment, something unusual in traditional society and even in Europe.

To the outsider, Rora is particularly important because it demonstrates all the key aspects of the new health services: the focus on serving the people as a whole, rather than a small minority as in so many other Third World countries; the unique participation through the health committee and through a continuous process of health education; a focus on primary health care and the care of pregnant women; a holistic approach which studies forest ecology and medicinally useful plants, and which through the traditional birth attendant demonstrates the preservation of what is good and useful in traditional society, accompanied by a scrupulous rejection of what is harmful.

However, as Dr Abrahed Gebre Kidan, head of the maternity

unit at Orota Hospital said, the situation in Rora is not representative of the country as a whole because Rora is an area where the EPLF has had an uninterrupted presence for many years. The broader picture is still one of acute suffering. The drought and famine have intensified malnutrition. Many women are weakened by lack of food from childhood onwards, since women eat only the left-overs of men, and girls in the crucial years of puberty are similarly deprived. Women are further weakened by an apparently endless series of pregnancies, with no time for the body to recover in between. Consequently, maternal mortality is distressingly high. In Semhar province, for example, one out of every poor women died within six months of childbirth. As Abrahed explained because of severe anaemia, even if a woman loses as little as 60–100 cc of blood she could go into shock and die.

The retraining of traditional birth attendants is helping to reduce the percentage of women who die during childbirth. Achievements in this field provide a model which can and should be applied elsewhere. The status, function and networks of these highly respected women have been preserved but their role has been transformed by training and equipping them. As Abrahed Gebre Kidan told me:

> There are two types of attendants – those who work only for their families, and some famous ones who go to different areas. No one delivers without a traditional birth attendant. But the traditional methods they use include a number of malpractices. For example, to initiate labour if there is inertia they massage the abdomen; they just put on some oil or butter and keep on massaging. That irritates the uterus and is the main cause of postpartal haemorrhage. The uterus gets angry and stops contracting when the baby is out. There are other things: for example, in the second stage of labour if there is a delay they start shaking and keep on shaking the whole body. They think this helps to shorten the delivery but it causes a lot of malaise and even malpresentation. Sometimes in the second stage of labour they do not look at the vulva to check if the baby's head is coming out; they pass their hand under the clothing and without looking, just by feeling, cut with sharp scissors. Sometimes they can

cut the baby's head. After that the baby needs surgery and there is a lot of bleeding for the mother.

Oh . . . the malpractices are uncountable, but then of course normal deliveries are in the majority and they have experience in handling these. What we are doing, in the areas where we can reach them, is training them, those of them who are not too old. They are trained in the areas where they live through health centres, health stations and mobile units. They are trained by an assistant midwife and given a modern delivery kit. Over three hundred have been trained now in April 1987, some in the liberated areas and some behind the enemy lines. We are really very proud of their work.

Watching the traditional birth attendants receiving their training at the Rora Health Centre, few of them young women and all of them traditionally dressed, I longed to talk to them to find out what they thought about the past and the future, with all their experience. Did the social change which their new role represented – undoubtedly an integral part of the revolution – also connect with and strengthen the armed struggle? But they were busy and we were moving on. Later in another area, however, I was to meet a woman whose wisdom, charm and powerful revolutionary consciousness were to inspire me for a long time. Fifty-year-old Abrahedsien Girmai is a member of the People's Assembly, has been an EPLF cadre since the early 1970s, and has also been for a major part of her life a traditional birth attendant in her village Fishae Merrara in Semniae Behare district. Her experiences bring out the dialectical relationship between health and self-defence, between survival and struggle, between personal and collective experience. She told me of her clandestine work with the EPLF, how her house and her village were surrounded by Ethiopian soldiers who had been sent to catch "the bandit Abrahedsein", and how she escaped disguised as a very old woman in a veil. She continued:

> Then in 1988 the village was bombarded with heavy artillery including a Stalin organ (BM21) which can fire 20 rockets at once. We had to flee. Many people died, old people and many mothers, some because of the Ethiopian attacks, some from sickness and

starvation. But some of us got here . . . The trip took four weeks: two weeks in hiding and two weeks on the way. Pregnant women were giving birth and because I am a birth attendant I was helping them. The children were given the names of places they were born in. On the way to Afabet the Ethiopians were chasing us. But the fighters intervened – they said: "You will never capture them!"

9 The Future

As I write this, in September 1990, many observers of the Eritrean situation are predicting that the next few months will bring the final victory for the Eritrean people. Between now and then political pressure will be brought to bear on the international community to recognize Eritrea and urge Mengistu to surrender. At the same time the besieged Ethiopian army in Asmara will become progressively more demoralized and the civilian population will be prepared for the inevitable battle if Mengistu does not surrender.

How do the fighters on the front line see it? Are they willing to speculate? In the past they have always refused to be drawn. Asked by foreign visitors when they think Eritrea will be liberated, they smile and say only: "we'll fight for as long as it takes", "our lives are like matches – they burn out and we have fulfilled our purpose". But now it seems that the day is finally almost here and every Eritrean is keenly aware of it: not only the 3 million people inside Eritrea who one way or another have been part of this struggle for 29 years, but also their mirror image, the large Eritrean community who fled from their towns and villages or were displaced for other reasons, and are now refugees outside the country in Sudan, the Middle East, Europe and America.

Hiwet Ogba Georgis (see page 15), now a domestic worker in Britain, has gone home already on a preliminary trip. "I'll feel so happy! so strong! I'll look 25!", she told me. "If we have our country, I don't care even if I am hungry or if I have no money – because already I have given everything for my land." There are others like her – domestic workers in Koln, Rome and Jeddah – who for years have sustained and secured the revolution with contributions from their meagre wages obtained under conditions hardly different from those of Italian colonialism. There is no doubt that they too will return as soon as they possibly can. There are also businessmen, academics, technicians, scientists, artists and many others in exile. There are – families whose babies and children of school-age are growing up in Europe and America. Many of them too support the struggle, through their membership of the unions, through solidarity work and through monthly contributions to the Eritrean People's Liberation Front (EPLF).

At the Eritrean festival in Bologna which is attended by around six thousand Eritreans every year I had the opportunity to meet some of this immense variety of people comprising the community of overseas Eritreans. For one week most of them stay in a huge camp-site while a minority find hotels. All day there are political programmes and cultural shows fraught with emotion, particularly when the performers are from the field. Then in the evening everyone returns to the camp-site and relaxes. Teenagers parade in the trendiest Italian fashions, parents walk around overwhelmed at meeting childhood friends not seen for years. Middle-aged women busy catering for the camp suddenly grab a long-lost friend and kiss repeatedly, first on one cheek and then the other. Intellectuals sit drinking and arguing in the bar. More and more people arrive. Groups of obviously "American" Eritreans in suits stand disconsolately at the entrance to the camp-site surveying the rudimentary accommodation while their wives look after piles of baggage containing more suits. An exquisitely outfitted "Canadian" Eritrean woman takes one look at the camp and then turns away: "My skin!" she says, delicately indicating her face, "it can't take this! – I'll have to go find a hotel."

Many of them will go back to Eritrea when the war is over. How will they manage, and more significantly, how will the country be affected by this new influx of skills and expectations? As we have seen Eritrea already has its own legal and administrative systems, educational and cultural institutes, health and education services, agricultural projects, and some of the basic essentials required for a self-reliant economy. However, the end of the armed struggle will bring not only the potential for more rapid development but far higher expectations, and not just among returning refugees but among those who have stayed on through the harsh experiences of war. Inevitably new issues will arise which will demand new strategies. For example, in the liberated zone distribution of all commodities has been largely controlled by the EPLF. How will the establishment of a cash economy affect power relations? If commercial markets are set up how will the EPLF handle the inevitable differentials which will emerge? What will the relationship between private employers and the state be? What role will foreign capital play, and how will it affect the people's culture? Some of these questions are only partially resolved.

According to Ande Michael Kahsai, one subject discussed at the 1987 Congress was that of foreign investment. It was decided that Eritrean nationals will be encouraged to invest in the private sector, and foreign capital will only be accepted in the public sector. "It means that we are consciously allowing capitalism to exploit in order to develop the economy – given the situation we cannot avoid it. The matter then will be how we limit the damage – through taxation and so on." How then will the system of welfare benefits be affected by the appearance of private owners and employers? Benefits such as maternity leave will be retained, Ande Michael said, because they are "fundamental rights which have been won through the struggle of women and their own sacrifices, and will have to be maintained". As for the structure of the state itself: "After all the experience [elsewhere], particularly that of Third World countries, we cannot have a one-party state. We have not specifically stated that it will be a multi-party system but I feel we will be moving towards it gradually." Can any economic and administrative structure, however equitable, sustain the improvements in the position of women which occurred in an atmosphere of unparalleled dynamism generated by the struggle for national liberation? In many other anti-colonial revolutions, particularly in Africa, independence did not fulfil the hopes the struggle had raised. How is Eritrea different?

On the one hand it is true that in many parts of the country, particularly those where the EPLF has not had a long and uninterrupted presence, women still face the oppression characteristic of a semi-feudal society.[49] Veiling is common, child marriage and infibulation are not infrequent, and women do not participate in politics. Even in areas where the EPLF has had a fairly long presence old attitudes remain, particularly among the older people. As Maharite Tekhle told me, confiding her preference for boy children over girls: "In the old days we were taught to prefer boys. It takes a long time to change; sometimes we find ourselves thinking in the old ways."

On the other hand in Eritrea there is a unique factor emerging from the extensive areas which have been under EPLF control for a decade and a half. Here a whole generation has grown up with the notion of women's equality. Many of these youngsters cannot remember the days before 1973 when there were no women fighters, or before 1977 when there were no people's assemblies, or when women did not defend their villages as people's militia. They know that women's emancipation is a priority taken on during the war and not shelved till after the revolution. The women of this new generation are fully equipped to carry on the struggle for women's emancipation. Just as they do not currently tolerate tokenism (for this reason there is no fixed number of seats for women in the Central Committee), they also do not romanticize "African culture" for the sake of it. They preserve what is positive about traditional culture and reject what is reactionary. And, perhaps because of the sacrifices they have made and the scale of their military and political participation, they have a strong sense of their democratic rights: they will demand that any future leaders of Eritrea will be accountable to them.

These young women and many older ones in the liberated areas have a strong sense of collective identity as women. Like Abrahedsien Girmai they believe that: "Women are fighting at the front, we too are fighting here and as a result we gain equal rights . . . in the future we are not going to give them up." They would be able and willing to fight oppressive measures brought by any future government. In this they would have the support of the National Union of Eritrean Women (NUEW) – an independent, dynamic and strong organization with branches all over the country, whose activities constantly reinforce women's collective identity and enhance the understanding that the struggle against sexism is a long-term one. It is struggle for which, as Askalu Menkarios said, "we have a strong foundation but there is still quite a long way to go". Because revolution is never perfect and complete, free Eritrea will not and cannot bring women's emancipation ready-made, it can merely be expected to tip the balance in favour of the oppressed. As Asmeret Abraham said, speaking about the work of her branch of the NUEW in strengthening women's position by organizing literacy classes and mobilizing women, often in the face of their husbands' opposition: "Once this war is over, once we get our country, we'll be able to do so much – our strength will be doubled! trebled!"

Appendix 1a The National Democratic Programme of the Eritrean People's Liberation Front, January 1977

Objectives

1. Establish a People's Democratic State

   A. Abolish the Ethiopian colonial administrative organs and all anti-national and undemocratic laws as well as nullify the military, economic and political treaties affecting Eritrea signed between colonial Ethiopia and other governments.
   B. Safeguard the interests of the masses of workers, peasants and other democratic forces.
   C. Set up a People's Assembly constituted of people's representatives democratically and freely elected from anti-feudal and anti-imperialist patriotic forces. The People's Assembly shall draw up the constitution, promulgate laws, elect the people's administration and ratify national economic plans and new treaties.
   D. Protect the people's democratic rights – freedom of speech, the press, assembly, worship and peaceful demonstration; develop anti-feudal and anti-imperialist worker, peasant, women, student and youth organisations.
   E. Assure all Eritrean citizens equality before the law without distinction as to nationality, tribe, region, sex, cultural level, occupation, position, wealth, faith, etc.
   F. Severely punish Eritrean lackeys of Ethiopian colonialism who have commited crimes against the nation and the people.

2. Build an Independent, Self-Reliant and Planned National Economy

A. Agriculture

1. Confiscate all land in the hands of the aggressor Ethiopian regime, the imperialist, zionists and Eritrean lackeys and put it in the service of the Eritrean masses.
2. Make big nationalised farms and extensive farms requiring modern techniques state-farms and use their produce for the benefit of the masses.
3. Abolish feudal land relations and carry out an equitable distribution of land. Strive to introduce cooperative farms by creating conditions of cooperation and mutual assistance so as to develop a modern and advanced system of agriculture and animal husbandry capable of increasing the income and improving the lot of the peasantry.
4. Induce the peasants to adopt modern agricultural techniques, introduce them to advanced agricultural implements and provide them with advisors, experts, veterinary services, fertilizers, wells, dams, transportation, finance, etc., in order to alleviate their problems and improve their livelihood and working conditions.
5. Provide the nomads with veterinary services, livestock breeding experts, agricultural advisors and financial assistance in order to enable them to lead settled lives, adopt modern techniques of agriculture and animal husbandry and improve their livelihood.
6. Provide for the peaceful and amicable settlement of land disputes and inequality among individuals and villages in such a way as to harmonize the interest of the aggrieved with that of the national economic interest.
7. Advance the economic and living conditions in, and bridge the gap between, the cities and the countryside.
8. Make pastures and forests state property, preserve wild life and forestry, and fight soil erosion.
9. Maintain a proper balance between agriculture and industry in the context of the planned economy.

10. Promote an association that will organise, politicise and arm the peasants with a clear revolutionary outlook so they can fully participate in the anti-colonial and anti-feudal struggle, defend the gains of the revolution, free themselves from oppression and economic exploitation, and manage their own affairs.

B. Industry

1. Nationalise all industries in the hands of the imperialists, zionists, Ethiopian colonialists and their Eritrean lackeys as well as resident aliens opposed to Eritrean independence.
2. Nationalise big industries, ports, mines, public transport, communications, power plants and other basic economic resources.
3. Exploit marine resources, expand the production of salt and other minerals, develop the fish industry, explore oil and other minerals.
4. Allow nationals who were not opposed to the independence of Eritrea to participate in national construction by owning small factories and workshops compatible with national development and the system of administration.
5. Strive to develop heavy industry so as to promote light industry, advance agriculture and combat industrial dependence.

C. Finance

1. Nationalise all insurance companies and banks, so as to centralise banking operations, regulate economic activities and accelerate economic development.
2. Establish a government-owned central national bank and issue an independent national currency.
3. Prohibit usury in all forms and extend credit at the lowest interest in order to eliminate the attendant exploitation of the masses.
4. Design and implement an appropriate tariffs policy to

secure the domestic market for the nation's agricultural, industrial and handicraft products.

5. Formulate and implement an equitable and rational taxation policy to administer and defend the country, carry out production and social functions.

D. Trade

1. Construct essential land, air and sea transportation and communications to develop the nation's trade.
2. Handle all import and export trade.
3. Nationalise the big trading companies and regulate the small ones.
4. Prohibit the export of essential commodities and limit the import of luxury goods.
5. Regulate the exchange and pricing of the various domestic products.
6. Strictly prohibit contraband trade.
7. Establish trade relations with all countries that respect Eritrean sovereignty irrespective of political systems.

E. Urban Land and Housing

1. Make urban land state property.
2. Nationalise all excess urban houses in order to abolish exploitation through rent and improve the livelihood of the masses.
3. Set, taking the standard of living into account, a rational rent price in order to improve the living conditions of the masses.
4. Compensate citizens for nationalised property in accordance with a procedure based on personal income and the condition of the national economy.
5. Build appropriate modern houses to alleviate the shortage of housing for the masses.

3. Develop Culture, Education, Technology and Public Health

A. Culture

1. Obliterate the decadent culture and disgraceful social habits that Ethiopian colonialism, world imperialism and zionism have spread in order to subjugate and exploit the Ethiopian people and destroy their identity.
2. In the new educational curriculum, provide for the proper dissemination, respect and development of the history of Eritrea and its people, the struggle against colonialism, oppression and for national independence, the experience, sacrifices and heroism as well as the national folklore, traditions and culture of the Eritrean people.
3. Destroy the bad aspects of the culture and traditions of Eritrean society and develop its good and progressive content.
4. Ensure that the Eritrean people glorify and eternally cherish the memory of heroic martyrs of the struggle for independence who, guided by revolutionary principles, gave their lives for the salvation of their people and country.

B. Education and Technology

1. Combat illiteracy to free the Eritrean people from the darkness of ignorance.
2. Provide for universal compulsory education up to the middle school.
3. Establish institutions of higher education in the various fields of science, arts, technology, agriculture, etc.
4. Grant students scholarships to pursue studies in the various fields of learning.
5. Establish schools in the various regions of Eritrea in accordance with the need.
6. Separate education from religion.
7. Make the state run all the schools and provide free education at all levels.

8. Integrate education with production and put it in the service of the masses.

9. Enable nationals, especially the students and youth, to train and develop themselves in the sciences, literature, handicrafts and technology through the formation of their own organisations.

10. Provide favourable work conditions for experts and the skilled to enable them to utilise their skills and knowledge in the service of the masses.

11. Engage in educational, cultural and technological exchange with other countries on the basis of mutual benefit and equality.

C. *Public Health*

1. Render medical services freely to the people.
2. Eradicate contagious diseases and promote public health by building the necessary hospitals and health centres all over Eritrea.
3. Scientifically develop traditional medicine.
4. Establish sports and athletic facilities and popularise them among the masses.

4. Safeguard Social Rights

A. *Worker's Rights*

1. Politicise and organise the workers, whose participation in the struggle had been hindered by the reactionary line and leaderships, and enable them in a higher and more organised form, to play their vanguard role in the revolution.

2. Abolish the system of labour laws and sham trade unions set up by Ethiopian colonialism and its imperialist masters to exploit and oppress Eritrean workers.

3. Enforce an eight-hour working day and protect the right of workers to rest for one day a week and twenty five days a year.

4. Promulgate a special labour code that properly protects the rights of workers and enables them to form unions.

5. Assure workers comfortable housing and decent living conditions.

6. Devise a social security programme to care for and assist workers, who, because of illness, disability or age, are unable to work.

7. Prohibit unjustified dismissals and undue pay cuts.

8. Protect the right of workers to participate in the management and administration of enterprises and industries.

9. Struggle to eliminate unemployment and protect every citizen's right to work.

B. Women's Rights

1. Develop an association through which women can participate in the struggle against colonial aggression and for social transformation.

2. Outline a broad programme to free woman from domestic confinement, develop their participation in social production, and raise their political, cultural and technical levels.

3. Assure women full rights of equality with men in politics, economy and social life as well as equal pay for equal work.

4. Promulgate progressive marriage and family laws.

5. Protect the right of women workers to two months' maternity leave with full pay.

6. Protect the rights of mothers and children, provide delivery, nursery and kindergarten services.

7. Fight to eradicate prostitution.

8. Respect the right of women not to engage in work harmful to their health.

9. Design programmes to increase the number and upgrade the quality of women leaders and public servants.

C. Families of Martyrs, Disabled Fighters and Others Needing Social Assistance

1. Provide necessary care and assistance to all fighters and other citizens who, in the course of the struggle against

Ethiopian colonialism and for national salvation, have suffered disability in jails or in armed combat.

2. Provide assistance and relief to the victims of Ethiopian colonial aggression, orphans, the old and the disabled as well as those harmed by natural causes.

3. Render necessary assistance and care for the families of martyrs.

5. Ensure the Quality and Consolidate the Unity of Nationalities

A. Abolish the system and laws instituted by imperialism, Ethiopian colonialism and their lackeys in order to divide, oppress and exploit the Eritrean people.

B. Rectify all errors committed by opportunists in the course of the struggle.

C. Combat national chauvinism as well as narrow nationalism.

D. Nurture and strengthen the unity and fraternity of Eritrean nationalities.

E. Accord all nationalities equal rights and responsibilities in leading them toward national progress and salvation.

F. Train cadres from all nationalities in various fields to assure common progress.

G. Safeguard the right of all nationalities to preserve and develop their spoken or written language.

H. Safegaurd the right of all nationalities to preserve and develop their progressive culture and traditions.

I. Forcefully oppose those who, in the pursuit of their own interest, create cliques on the basis of nationality, tribe, region, etc, and obstruct the unity of the revolution and the people.

6. Build a Strong People's Army

A. Liberate the land and the people step by step through the strategy of people's war. Build a strong land, air and naval force capable of defending the country's borders, territorial waters, air space and territorial integrity as well as the full independence, progress and dignity of its people in order to attain prosperity and reach the highest economic stage. The people's army shall be:

– politically conscious, imbued with comradely relations, steeled through revolutionary discipline,
– full of resoluteness, imbued with a spirit of self-sacrifice, participating in production, and
– equipped with modern tactics, weapons and skills. Being the defender of the interests of the workers and peasants, it serves the entire people of Eritrea irrespective of religion, nationality or sex. The basis of this army is the revolutionary force presently fighting for national independence and liberation.

B. Establish a people's militia to safeguard the gains of the revolution and support the People's Army in the liberated and semi-liberated areas.

C. Establish a progressive and advanced military academy.

7. Respect Freedom of Religion and Faith

A. Safeguard every citizen's freedom of religion and belief.
B. Completely separate religion from the state and politics.
C. Separate religion from education and allow no compulsory religious education.
D. Strictly oppose all the imperialist-created new counter-revolutionary faiths, such as Jehovas' Witness, Pentecostal, Bahai, etc.
E. Legally punish those who try to sow discord in the struggle and undermine the progress of the Eritrean people on the basis of religion whether in the course of the armed struggle or in a people's democratic Eritrea.

8. Provide Humane Treatment to Prisoners of War and Encourage the Desertion of Eritrean Soldiers Serving the Enemy

A. Oppose the efforts of Ethiopian colonialism to conscript duped soldiers to serve as tools of aggression for the oppression and slaughter of the Eritrean people.

B. Encourage Eritrean soldiers and plainclothesmen who have been duped into serving in the Ethiopian colonial army to return to the just cause and join their people in the struggle against Ethiopian aggression and welcome them to its ranks with full right of equality.

C. Provide humane treatment and care for Ethiopian war prisoners.

D. Severely punish the die-hard, criminal and atrocious henchmen and lackeys of Ethiopian colonialism.

9. Protect the Rights of Eritreans Residing Abroad

A. Struggle to organise Eritreans residing abroad in the already formed mass organisations so they can participate in the patriotic anti-colonial struggle.

B. Strive to secure the rights of Eritrean refugees in the neighbouring countries, win them the assistance of international organisations, and work for the improvement of their living conditions.

C. Welcome nationals who want to return to their country and participate in their people's daily struggles and advances.

D. Encourage the return and create the means of the rehabilitation of Eritreans forced to flee their country and land by the vicious aggression and oppression of Ethiopian colonialism.

10. Respect the Rights of Foreigners Residing in Eritrea

A. Grant full rights of residence and work to aliens who have openly or covertly supported the Eritrean people's struggle against Ethiopian colonial oppression and for national salvation and are willing to live in harmony with the legal system to be established.

B. Mercilessly punish aliens who, as lackeys and followers of Ethiopian colonialism, imperialism and zionism, spy on or become obstacles to the Eritrean people.

11. Pursue a Foreign Policy of Peace and Non-Alignment

A. Welcome the assistance of any country or organisation which recognises and supports the just struggle of the Eritrean people without interference in its internal affairs.

B. Establish diplomatic relations with all countries irrespective of political and economic system on the basis of the following five principles:
- Respect for each other's independence, territorial integrity, and national sovereignty;
- Mutual non-aggression;
- Non-interference in internal affairs;
- Equality and mutual benefit;
- Peaceful co-existence.

C. Establish good friendly relations with all neighbours.

D. Expand cultural, economic and technological ties with all countries of the world compatible with national sovereignty and independence based on equality. Do not align with any world military bloc or allow the establishment of any foreign military bases on Eritrean soil.

E. Support all just and revolutionary movements, as our struggle is an integral part of the international revolutionary movement in general, and the struggle of the African, Asian and Latin American peoples agains colonialism, imperialism, zionism and racial discrimination in particular.

VICTORY TO THE MASSES!

Adopted by the First Congress of the EPLF on January 31st, 1977

Appendix 1b   National Democratic Programme of the Eritrean People's Liberation Front, March 1987

Objectives

1. Establish a People's Democratic State

   A. Abolish the Ethiopian colonial administrative organs and all anti-national and undemocratic laws and cancel the military economic, political and cultural treaties affecting Eritrea signed between the colonial power, Ethiopia, and other governments.
   B. Establish a state that safeguards the interests of the people and does not serve those of foreign forces.
   C. Constitute a People's Assembly through a free and democratic election of people's representatives. The People's Assembly shall draw the Constitution, passive laws, formulate policies, ratify new treaties and elect popular executive and judicial organs.
   D. Protect the democratic rights of freedom of speech, the press, assembly, worship and peaceful demonstration as well as the right of nationalist political parties and nationalist associations of workers, peasants, women, students, youth and professionals.
   E. Assure all Eritrean nationals equality before the law without distinction as to nationality, sex, affiliation, cultural level, occupation, position, wealthy, faith, etc.
   F. Punish severely Eritrean lackeys of Ethiopian colonialism who have committed crimes against their country and people.

2. Build an Independent, Self-Reliant and Planned National Economy

To develop the Eritrean economy there shall be private and public sectors in agriculture, industry and trade. The basic economic resources shall be state owned. Domestic capital investment in the private sector and foreign capital investment in the public sector shall be allowed and encouraged.

A. Agriculture

1. Put all land in the hands of the aggressor Ethiopian regime in the service of the Eritrean people.
2. Convert big farms requiring modern techniques into state farms and use their produce for the benefit of the people.
3. Implement an equitable distribution of land to make the land benefit the tiller.
4. Encourage the peasants to adopt modern agricultural techniques, introduce them to advanced agricultural implements and provide them with advisors, experts, veterinary services, fertilizers, wells, dams, transportation, finance, etc., to alleviate their problems and improve their livelihood and working conditions.
5. Provide the nomads with livestock breeding, veterinary and agricultural education as well as advisors, experts and financial assistance to enable them to lead settled lives, adopt modern means of animal husbandry and agriculture and improve their livelihood.
6. Provide for the peaceful and amicable settlement of land disputes and inequity among individuals and villages in such a way as to harmonize the interest of the aggrived party with that of national construction.
7. Advance the economic and living conditions in, and bridge the gap between, the cities and the countryside.
8. Make extensive pastures and forests public property, preserve wild life and forestry and conduct a campaign of reforestation.
9. Maintain a proper balance between agriculture and industry in economic planning.

B. Industry

1. Nationalize all industries in the hands of Ethiopian colonialists, its Eritrean collaborators and foreigners hostile to Eritrean independence.
2. Nationalize big industries, mines, marine resources, communication, public transport and power plants.
3. Exploit marine resources, expand the production of salt and other minerals, develop the fish industry and explore available minerals.
4. Encourage Eritreans with capital to participate in national construction by setting up factories and enterprises in the private sector.
5. Strive to develop heavy industry so as to promote light industry, advance agriculture and combat industrial dependence.

C. Finance

1. Centralize banking and put all insurance companies and banks under the state to regulate economic activities and accelerate economic development.
2. Establish a state owned central national bank and issue an independent national currency.
3. Prohibit usury in all its forms and extend credit at low interest to save the people from exploitation.
4. Design and implement an appropriate tariffs policy to protect the domestic market for the nation's agricultural, industrial and handicraft products.
5. Formulate and implement an equitable and rational taxation policy to provide for the administration and defence of the country, sustenance of productive activities and the extension of social services.

D. Trade

1. Extend a network of land, air and sea communications and transport essential to develop the nation's trade.
2. There shall be state and private trade and the state shall regulate private trade to ensure its compatibility with national construction.
3. Ban the export of essential consumer goods and limit the import of luxury items.
4. Regulate the exchange and pricing of the various domestic products.
5. Strictly prohibit contraband trade.
6. Establish trade relations with all countries irrespective of political systems.

E. Urban Land and Housing

1. Make all urban land public property with leasing allowed under state regulation.
2. Review the incorrect nationalization of houses carried out by the Dergue.
3. Every national will be allowed to build houses for residence and rent.
4. Set a rational rent price that takes into account the prevailing standard of living in order to improve the people's livelihood.
5. Build houses as needed through modernplans to alleviate the shortage of housing and solve the problem of the people.

3. Develop Culture, Education, Technology and Public Health

A. Culture

1. Destroy the decadent alien cultures and disgraceful social habits spread by Ethiopian colonialism and other foreign forces to subjugate and exploit the Eritrean people and destroy their identity.

2. Eliminate the bad aspects of the cultures and traditions of Eritrean society and develop their good and positive contents.

3. Provide, through the educational opportunities accorded the Eritrean people, for the proper awareness, respect and development of the history of Eritrea and its people, of the struggle against colonialism, oppression and for national independence, of the sacrifices and heroism as well as of the national folklore, tradition, and culture of the Eritrean people.

4. Ensure that the Eritrean people remain proud and always cherish the memory of the heroic martyrs of the struggle for freedom and independence who, loyal to their revolutionary ideals, gave their lives for the salvation of their people and country.

5. Establish cultural centres, clubs and facilities, such as theatres, cinemas, etc., to develop a progressive national culture.

B. *Education and Technology*

The educational policy of the EPLF aims to secure the development of industry, agriculture and technology in order to improve the livelihood of the people; to narrow and eliminate the gap in the levels of cultural development; and promote the national unity of the Eritrean people.

1. Combat illiteracy to free the Eritrean people from the darkness of ignorance.

2. Provide for universal compulsory education up to the middle school; each nationality may give elementary education in its own language or any other language of its choice.

3. Establish institutions of higher education in the various fields of science, arts, technology and agriculture; English shall be the language of instruction in education above the elementary level.

4. Teach Arabic as a subject at all levels of education.

5. Grant students scholarships to pursue studies in the various fields of learning.

6. Establish schools in the various parts of Eritrea, with special focus on the regions where education is not widespread.
7. Separate education from religion.
8. Provide free state education at all levels.
9. Integrate education with production and put it in the service of the people.
10. Enable nationals, especially the students and youth, to train and develop themselves in the sciences, literature, handicrafts and technology through the formation of their own associations.
11. Provide favourable work conditions for experts and the skilled to enable them to utilize their skills and knowledge in the service of the people.
12. Engage in educational, cultural and technological exchange with other countries on the basis of mutual benefit and equality.

C. Public Health

1. Strive to provide free health care for all the people.
2. Eradicate diseases and promote public health by building hospitals and health centres as needed all over Eritrea.
3. Develop the country's traditional medicine through the application of scientific methods.
4. Establish sports and athletic facilities to cultivate a healthy population.

4. Safeguard Social Rights

A. Workers' Rights

1. Provide for the highest degree of organization of the workers and the raising of their productive potential as they are the ones who shoulder the heaviest tasks for the development of the country's industry and agriculture.
2. Abolish the administration, laws and sham trade unions set up by Ethiopian colonialism and its collaborators to exploit and oppress Eritrean workers.

3. Limit an eight-hour working day and protect the right of workers to rest one day a week and twenty five working days a year.

4. Promulgate a special labour code thay duly protects the rights of workers.

5. Assure workers comfortable housing and decent living conditions.

6. Devise a programme of social security to care for and assist workers who, because of illness, disability or age, are unable to work.

7. Prohibit unjustified dismissals and undue pay-cuts.

8. Provide for the participation of workers in the management and administration of the enterprises in which they work.

9. Struggle to eliminate unemployment.

B. *Women's Rights*

1. Develop a union through which women can participate in the struggle for national liberation and for social transformation.

2. Outline a broad programme to free women from domestic confinement and raise their political, cultural and productive levels.

3. Assure women full rights of equality with men in politics, the economy and social life as well as equal pay for similar work.

4. Promulgate marriage and family laws that safeguard the rights of women.

5. Protect the right of women to two months' maternity leave with full pay.

6. Protect the rights of mothers and children and provide delivery nursery and kindergarten services.

7. Struggle to eradicate prostitution.

8. Respect the right of women not to engage in work harmful to their health.

9. Design programmes to increase the number and upgrade the quality of women leaders and public servants.

C. Families of Martyrs, Disabled Fighters and Others Needing Social Assistance

1. Provide necessary care and assistance to all fighters and other nationals who, in the course of the struggle against Ethiopian colonialism and for national salvation, have suffered disability in combat or in jails.
2. Provide assistance and relief to the victims of Ethiopian colonial aggression, orphans, the old and the disabled as well as those harmed by natural causes.
3. Provide appropriate education and training programmes to disabled nationals so as to make them productive.
4. Render necessary assistance and care for the families of martyrs.

5. Ensure the Equality and Consolidate the Unity of Nationalities

A. Abolish the administrative systems, practices, laws, instituted by Ethiopian colonialism and others to divide, oppress and exploit the Eritrean people.

B. Rectify all errors committed by opportunists in the course of the struggle.

C. Combat national chauvinism and narrow nationalism.

D. Nurture and strengthen the unity and fraternity of Eritrean nationalities.

E. Accord all nationalities equal rights and responsibilities in leading them toward national progress and salvation.

F. Train cadres from all nationalities in various fields to assure common development.

G. Safeguard the right of all nationalities to preserve and develop their spoken or written language.

H. Encourage all nationalities to preserve and develop the positive aspects of their cultures and traditions.

I. Oppose individuals or groups who, for the sake of their parochial interests, create sectarian groups on the basis of nationality, tribe, province, etc., and obstruct the unity of the revolution and the people.

J. Each nationality may establish its own democratic administrative organ or organs compatible with its specific conditions.

6. Build a Strong People's Army

A. Pursue in the armed struggle for national liberation, the military strategy of people's war to liberate the people and the land step by step.

B. Build regional armies and people's militia forces to safeguard the gains of the revolution in the liberated and semi-liberated areas.

C. Build strong land, air and naval forces capable of defending the country's borders, territorial waters and air space as well as safeguarding the territorial integrity, full independence, progress and dignity of the Eritrean people so as to attain prosperity and the highest economic level of society. The people's army shall be:
Politically mature, enjoying comradely relations and steeled through revolutionary discipline;
Resolute, imbued with a spirit of self-sacrifice and productive, and
Equipped with modern tactics, weapons and skills.
As the defender of the people, it serves the entire peopel of Eritrea irrespective of religion, nationality or sex. The basis of this army shall be the revolutionary force presently fighting for national independence and liberation.

D. Establish an advanced military academy.

7. Respect Freedom of Religion and Faith

A. Safeguard the freedom of religion and belief of every national.

B. Separate religion from the state and politics.

C. Bar religious education from all schools while allowing clerical institutions to provide only religious education.

D. Punish those who, whether during the armed struggle or in a people's democratic Eritrea, try to undermine the struggle and progress of the Eritrean people through religious discord.

8. Provide Humane Treatment to Prisoners of War and Encourage the Desertion of Eritrean Soldiers Serving the Enemy

A. Oppose the efforts of Ethiopian colonialism to forcibly conscript soldiers to serve as tools of its aggression to oppress and crush the Eritrean people.

B. Encourage Eritrean soldiers and "bandas" who have been forced to serve in the Ethiopian colonial army to return to the just cause and join their people in the struggle against Ethiopian aggression and welcome them with full rights of equality.

C. Provide humane treatment to Ethiopian prisoners of war, make them aware of the justness of the Eritrean cause, provide them with education and professional training, set them free and help them return to peaceful life in their country.

D. Punish severely the die-hard, criminal and loyal servants of Ethiopian colonialism.

9. Protect the Rights of Eritreans Resident Abroad

A. Struggle to create conditions for Eritreans resident abroad to join the armed struggle against Ethiopian colonialism, participate in the mass organizations and professional associations set up and, as Eritrean communities, safeguard their culture, identity and rights and strengthen their mutual co-operation.

B. Strive to protect the rights of Eritrean refugees, win them assistance from governments and international organizations and improve their social conditions.

C. Encourage them to return to their country and become participants in their country's daily struggle and development.

D. Conduct efforts for the voluntary repatriation and rehabilitation in the liberated areas of Eritreans who have been forced to free their land and country by the vicious aggression and oppression of Ethiopian colonialism.

10. Respect the Rights of Foreigners Resident in Eritrea

A. Grant full rights of residence, work permit and citizenship on demand in accordance with the immigration laws to aliens who have openly or covertly supported the Eritrean people's struggle against Ethiopian colonialism and its collaborators and have not worked against the revolution provided that they wish to live in harmony with the legal system to be established.

B. Punish mercilessly resident foreigners who, as collaborators, lackeys or followers of Ethiopian colonialism, spy on or become obstacles to the Eritrean people.

C. Punish legally resident aliens who become tools of any hostile foreign power.

11. Pursue a Foreign Policy of Peace and Non-Alignment

A. Present appeals to the United Nations and its member states and conduct diplomatic activities to assert the legitimate right of the Eritrean people.

B. Welcome the assistance of any country or organization which recognizes and supports the just struggle of the Eritrean people without interference in its internal affairs.

C. Establish diplomatic relations with all countries irrespective of political and economic systems on the basis of the following five principles:

Respect for independence, territorial integrity and national sovereignty;
Mutual non-aggression;
Non-interference in internal affairs;
Working for equality and mutual benefit; and
Peaceful coexistence.

D. Establish good friendly relations with all neighbours.

E. Expand cultural, economic and technological ties with all countries consistent with national sovereignty and independence and based on equality, without aligning with any global military organization or allowing the establishment of any foreign military base on Eritrean soil.

F. Support all just and democratic movements, as our struggle is an integral part of the struggle of the world's peoples, in general, and the struggles of the African, Asian, and

Latin American peoples against world colonialism, foreign intervention and racism in particular.

G. Become a member of various international and regional organizations consistent with the identity and independence of Eritrea.

Victory to the Masses!
March 1987

Appendix 2   Facts About Students and Schools in Eritrea

- Schools are run by the Department of Education, which has eight zones and three boards which handle vocational training, curriculum development and adult education.
- Eritrean Relief Association administers nine schools in eastern Sudan.
- The Education Department administers 135 schools in Eritrea.
- Eritrea students have a history of resistance to domination which has made them special targets of Ethiopian repression for 30 years. In the late 1950s, a wave of student strikes protesting the use of Amharic in the schools resulted in mass jailing of students. Tens of thousands of Eritrean students died in the so-called Red Terror campaign of 1977.
- Traditionally, girls were largely prevented from getting a basic education, resulting in a 90% illiteracy rate among Eritrean women. Now education of girls is considered a top priority.
- Eritrean high school and university graduates have a diversity of educational experiences. They have gone to Koranic and Christian mission schools; their teachers have been members of the U.S. Peace Corps, Indians and Britons. They have studied in Asmara, the capital of Eritrea, as well as in Ethiopia, the Middle East, Europe and North America.
- A new technical school for the teaching of vocational skills opened in Wina, Eritrea, in 1985.

Source: Eritrean Relief Association (London, 1986)

Appendix 3 Development of the ELF from 1981 onwards

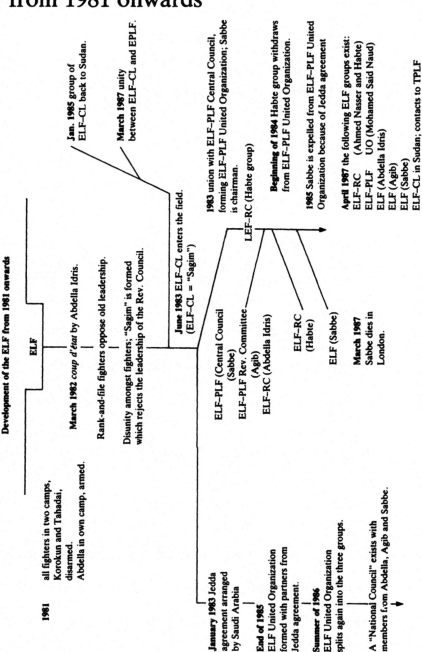

Source: Zemberet Yohannes, former member of the ELF–CL leadership, now EPLF cc member.

Appendix 4   Policy of Land Redistribution Formulated by the Eritrean People's Liberation Front[18]

1. All the farming land in the area where land redistribution is to take place should first be put in the hands of the inhabitants of the area and its transformation into Diesa tenure proclaimed. It should then be prepared for redistribution.
2. The factors of distance and fertility having been taken into consideration, land should then be distributed equally at the level of families eligible for such allocation of land.
3. Only those with married status and who fulfil their duties and responsibilities may be allocated land.
4. In special situations (eg when an applicant is too poor to marry or is physically disadvantaged) unmarried applicants above the age of twenty five may receive half of the plot allotted to a family.
5. Families formed after redistribution (wareda) has already been undertaken may recieve their plot of land one year after marriage.
6. The right of women to own land is fully recognised and protected.
6.1 In the event of a divorce, the land is divided between the parties equitably.
6.2 Widows and their children receive full rights to land allocation.

Appendix 4   181

6.3   A childless woman receives half of a family plot.

6.4   A woman past the age of marriage (a spinster) receives half of a family plot.

6.5   A woman past the age of 25 who is unfit for marriage and who may live with her family or relations receives half of a family plot.

6.6   A woman who comes back to her village on being divorced, may according to her choice, receive land in her home or her husband's village.

7.   Orphans may, according to their need, be allocated full or half of a family plot.

8.   The so-called "maikelai aliet" and the issues of a female villager have an equal claim to a share of village land.

9.   Villagers who previously held land but who live elsewhere in Eritrea, may if present on the date of redistribution (wareda) be *considered* for an allotment of a plot of land.

10.   Villagers living outside of Eritrea may not receive village land. However their rights will be protected upon their return.

11.   A married member (a fighter) of the People's Army's right to a claim of village land is fully protected. However if his family are under the direct care of the Front, such a claim is waived.

12.   Villagers serving as enemy soldiers are barred from any claim for land. However such a bar will be lifted on their return.

13.   Land may be owned in only one village.

14.   Land may neither be sold nor exchanged.

15.   The following plots of land may neither be farmed nor distributed.

15.1   Land reserved for cemeteries.

15.2   Construction sites

15.3   Forest areas

15.4   Land left fallow

15.5   Country roads

15.6   Land commonly used by the village community (e.g. the *baite*, or village assembly plot)

16. The village assembly decides on areas reserved for constructions.
17. Land belonging to members of the People's Militia, to fighters of the EPLF, to the aged and handicapped, to women and to those living outside the village is collectively farmed and managed by the local people's assembly. The people's assembly shall assign productive teams to farm the land. (From: *Creating a Popular, Economic, Political and Military Base*, EPLF (unpublished) 1982.)

Appendix 5   Organizational Structure of the Eritrean People's Liberation Front (EPLF) and Women's Representation (*March* 1987)

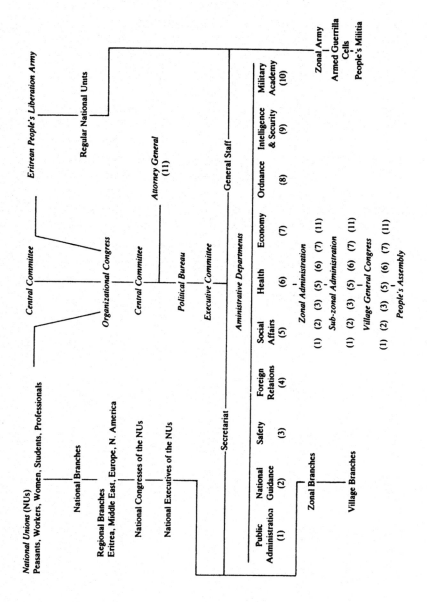

Notes on Women's Representation

* The Executive Committee of the National Union of Eritrean Women (NUEW) attends the Organizational Congress directly. It aims to be composed entirely of civilians but currently consists of a mixture of civilians and EPLF cadres.
* In addition, every hundred women elect one woman to go to the Congress. Anyone can be elected, the only condition being that she must have been in the EPLF or in the mass organizations for at least two years.
* The Congress reminds people to take into consideration the minority nationalities.
* Of those attending the Congress, from each department within the EPLF there is positive discrimination for women: 80% of the seats are contested with no stipulations, and the remaining 20% are filled by women voted in by men and women. This applies only to the EPLF because civilian women have the NUEW to represent them.
* There is no positive discrimination for women on the Central Committee because it is thought that this could lead to tokenism. Currently 6 of the 71 Central Committee members are women.

Appendix 6a   Eritrean People's Liberation Front Marriage Laws

CHAPTER ONE
GENERAL PRINCIPLES

Article 1

The feudal marriage norm based on the supremacy of men over women, haphazard and coercive arrangements, and which does not safeguard the welfare of children shall be banned.

The new democratic marriage law based on the free choice of both partners, monogamy, the equal rights of both sexes and the legal guarantees of the interests of women and children shall be implemented.

Article 2

Polygamy, concubinacy, the betrothal of children, interference in the re-marriage of widows as well as dowry and other gifts connected with marriage shall be abolished.

CHAPTER TWO
THE MARRIAGE LAW

Article 3

Marriage must be based on the absolute will of the two partners. Neither partner should use any form of pressure. Nor should any third party interfere in the matter.

Article 4
> The marriage contract shall be invoked only for males at the age of 20 or above and for females at the age of 18 or above.

Article 5
> If any of the following situations prevails, then the male or female shall be prevented from marriage:
> a. if the partners are of the same blood type or members of the same family;
> b. if one partner is incapacitated from sexual potency due to some physical infirmity;
> c. if one partner is afflicted by veneral diseases, disease of the brain, leprosy, or any other disease that is deemed by medical science as preventing marriage.

Article 6
> To effect the marriage contract, both partners must register with the central zonal administration of the locality they live in. If the marriage is in harmony with the legal requirements laid-down in this law, the central zonal administration shall expressly issue the partners the marriage certificates.

CHAPTER THREE

THE RIGHTS AND DUTIES OF THE HUSBAND AND WIFE

Article 7
> The husband and wife are companions sharing the same life. They ought to have equal status in their household.

Article 8
> It is the duty of the husband and wife to respect and love each other, to help and care for each other, to live in harmony, to participate in productive work, to look after their children and to endeavour in unison for the

welfare of the family as well as the promotion of a new society.

Article 9
Both partners have the right of a free choice of profession/ employment as well as a free participation in their work or other social activities.

Article 10
Both husband and wife must have the same rights as regards ownership and management of family property.

Article 11
The husband and wife shall have the mutual right to inherit each other's property.

CHAPTER FOUR
RELATIONS BETWEEN PARENTS AND CHILDREN

Article 12
Parents have the duty to upbring and educate their children. It is in turn incumbent upon the children to support and help their parents. Parents and children must not antagonise and betray each other.

Article 13
Parents and children have the mutual right of inheritance of their properties.

Article 14
Children born out of wedlock shall have the same rights as children born in legal marriage. No one is allowed to harm or discriminate against them.

When the paternity of a child born out of wedlock is legally asserted by his mother, other witnesses or other material evidence, the father shall bear the full or partial costs for the upbringing and education of the child until the age of 18.

Through the permission of the mother, the natural

father may take the responsibility for the direct upbringing of the child.
If the mother remarries, the legal contents of Article 21 concerning the upbringing of a child born out of wedlock shall apply.

Article 15

The husband and wife should not maltreat or discriminate against children born from a previous marriage.

CHAPTER FIVE

DIVORCE

Article 16

Divorce is permitted if both husband and wife seek it. In the circumstances in which either the husband or wife request it unilaterally, divorce shall be permitted only when reconciliation proves unattainable after the mediation of the zonal administration and other legal bodies. When both the husband and wife desire to initiate the process of divorce, they must both apply to the central zonal administration in order to obtain the relevant divorce certificates. The zonal administration shall subsequently issue the divorce certificates without undue delay after ascertaining that divorce is sought by both parties and having taken the necessary measures concerning the settlement of children and property.

In the case of one party only seeking divorce, the central zonal administration may endeavour to bring about reconciliation. If the mediation proves a failure, the issue shall be referred without delay to the Political Bureau for a decision. The central zonal administration should not attempt to hinder or obstruct any of the parties from appealing to the Political Bureau. The Political Bureau ought to attempt to bring about the reconciliation of the two parties when notified on the divorce issue. If the mediation fails, it shall give its verdict without delay.

If the divorcees wish to revive their married relations anew later, they have to apply to the central zonal administration for registration for marriage. The central zonal administration shall endorse the registration and issue a second marriage certificate.

Article 17

The husband cannot apply for divorce while the wife is a mother. He can only apply for divorce after the baby exceeds 1 year of age. This stricture does not apply in the case when it is the wife who seeks divorce.

Article 18

For a member of the People's Army who is in active service, he/she must first obtain the consent of his/her partner before he/she applies for divorce if he/she has been maintaining a steady contact through letters with his/her family. Divorce shall be permitted if he/she has not written a letter to his/her family for over two years before this law becomes effective and continues not to attempt to contact his/her family for one year after its effectiveness.

CHAPTER SIX

THE UPBRINGING AND EDUCATION OF CHILDREN AFTER DIVORCE

Article 19

The blood relation that obtains between parents and their children cannot be smeared by divorce. If either the father or mother assumes custody in rearing the children, this does not have any bearing and they would yet remain the children of both parents. After divorce both parents have the duty to look after and educate their children.

After divorce, the permission for the mother to take the responsibility of custodianship of an infant yet on breast-feeding is a central principle. After the baby ceases being breast-fed and if a conflict arises between the two parties regarding his custody and no accord reached between them, the central zonal administration shall settle the matter on the basis of the interest of the child.

Article 20

After divorce, if the mother is given the responsibility of rearing the child, the father shall bear the full or partial costs for the upbringing and education of the child. The amount and duration necessary for the upbringing and education of the child shall be determined by both parties. In the event that they disagree, the Political Bureau shall give its verdict.

Payment may be made through monetary, in kind or by tilling the land allotted to the child.

Such portion determined through the agreement of the parents or by a legal decision through the intervention of the central zonal administration relative to the upbringing and education of a child, does not preclude the child from requesting any of the parents for an increment in the financial allotment determined through parental agreement or by a legal ruling.

Article 21

If a divorced woman remarries anew and if her husband is willing to fully or partially bear the costs for the upbringing and education of her child or children, the father of the child or children has the right for a reduction of this cost for education and upbringing or a total exemption depending on the circumstances that prevail.

CHAPTER SEVEN
PROPERTY AND UPBRINGING AFTER DIVORCE

Article 22

If divorce takes place, the woman shall be entitled to appropriate the property she owned before her marriage. Other property of the family shall be shared through the consent of both parties. In regard to items for which an agreement of the parties cannot be reached, the central zonal administration shall settle the matter taking into consideration the actual condition of the property of the family, the interests of the wife and child or children and the principle of the utilization for the development of production.

If the portion of property allotted for the wife and her child or children is adequate for the rearing and education of the child or children, the husband may be exempted from bearing an additional rearing and educational cost.

Article 23

Any debt that the partners may have owed during their married life shall be paid from the property that the husband and wife had acquired in that period. In the event that they do not own any property or if what they own cannot compensate their debt, then the husband ought to bear the responsibility for settling this debt. The settlement of debts accruing solely to the husband or wife shall be the responsibility of the concerned party.

Article 24

After divorce, if one party does not get remarried and is afflicted by problems of survival, the other party ought to provide assistance. If both parties fail to agree on the modalities and duration of the assistance to be granted, the central zonal administration shall give its verdict.

CHAPTER EIGHT

POINTS THAT MUST BE SATISFIED IN THE SPECIAL CONDITIONS OF MARRIAGE BETWEEN TWO ARMED FIGHTERS

Article 25
>The marriage contract between two armed fighters can be invoked only when, in addition to the conditions stipulated in Articles 3 to 6, the partners have at least two years of experience in the armed struggle.

Article 26
>When two armed fighters apply for marriage, the central zonal administration shall issue a marriage certificate ascertaining that the marriage is in harmony with the legal contents of this law after 3 months of study.

THE CONDITIONS OF THE MARRIED

Article 27
>After marriage, the armed fighters shall be bestowed 30 days of honeymoon either in a place permitted or arranged by the Front or in a place in the field chosen by the couple themselves.

Article 28
>Two married armed fighters shall have either one week in six months or, cumulatively, two weeks a year of vacation together in accordance with their choice. Apart from these periods, permission shall be granted in the interim if they so request only in the event that their problem cannot be resolved otherwise.

Article 29
>The place or conditions of work of two married armed fighters is not decided by them but by the organization.

Article 30

An armed woman fighter shall have a leave of one month before and one month after her giving birth. When a fighter is pregnant, she shall be assigned to a place where she can work without hazard to her health.

GIVING BIRTH AND REARING OF CHILDREN

Article 31

Child rearing shall be the responsibility of the mother until our organization establishes kindergartens. Contraceptive orientation and instruction shall be given by medical doctors but abortion is absolutely prohibited.

CONCLUSION

Article 32

This marriage law shall be effective from the date that it is ratified by the Central Committee. It may be amended and developed from time to time through corrections effected by the Central Committee.

Appendix 6b Outline of the 1980 Seminar on Marriage

Courtship

Theoretical issues
How has the question of love been perceived and handled in different societies?

How does love develop from a simple biological or instinctual feeling into something psychological, emotional and intellectual?

Is love only the concern of the two individuals?

In the different historical stages in the development of society when did love start to be legitimate? When was it a sin and a crime?

Morality is part of ideology, ideology is part of the superstructure and in order to change the superstructure the economic base of the old society must be completely destroyed. Does this mean that you cannot begin to develop a new morality before you have established the complete domination of the new class?

Are all sexual relationships based in love? How do you differentiate between a sexual relationship based in love and one not based in love? What mental, material and emotional demands are placed on the people involved?

Is there an inherent limit on love in the proletarian ideology?

How will love be seen and what place will it have in a classless society?

Eritrean society
As Eritrean society is feudo-capitalist what attitudes do you find to sexual relationships and love?

Do you ever find sexual relationships and love before marriage? If you do, in what situations and with what result?

As Eritrean society is feudo-capitalist it has a feudo-bourgeois mentality and therefore men and women often base their relationships in material or status interests. What are these material and status interests?

Eritrean society, like all others, has laws governing sexual morals. Are these laws followed by everyone? Who violates them? Why? With what consequences?

Is pre-marital sex permitted in our society? If yes, under what conditions? What are the consequences of this?

How much influence have we had in changing people's attitudes in the liberated areas?

EPLF
What attitudes did male EPLF fighters have before women joined the struggle? Why did they have these attitudes and were there fighters who had relationships with civilians? If yes, what kind of relationships? Under what conditions did they have the relationship and with what result?

What was the attitude of male fighters when women started to join the armed struggle? How did those who had left their wives in the villages feel?

Why were sexual relationships prohibited before the 1st Congress of the EPLF? Were sexual relationships prohibited because the EPLF was against them or because of the morality of the time? How was celibacy enforced?

Were there people who violated the rule of celibacy? If there were, what sort of people were they?

At that time what was the basis of these people's relationships? Did they have the chance to get to know one another?

How many of the people who were having illicit sexual relationships do you think were found out? After they were found out what political, psychological and social consequences did they face?

Were these hidden relationships based in love or not? Do you think that most of these hidden relationships were successful or did they end?

Now that sexual relationships are permitted what criteria are women fighters using to choose their partner:

> his position?
> his political outlook?
> his physical appearance?
> emotional attachment?
> others?

How do you differentiate these criteria from those in the previous society and why? What shortcomings can be seen? Now that sexual relationships are permitted what criteria are men fighters using to choose their partner:

> physical appearance?
> political attitude?
> physical attraction?
> emotion attachment?
> others?

How do you differentiate these criteria from those in the previous society and why? What shortcomings can be seen?

Do we find love through calculation? Does every relationship end in marriage? Why? What shortcomings can we see in the EPLF with regard to sexual relationships?

Most relationships end on the initiative of the man. What reasons does he give for ending a relationship:

> the woman's political attitude?
> her character?
> sexual incompatability?
> because he discovers something about her he didn't know before?
> because he is infatuated with someone else?
> different places of assignment?
> others?

If a relationship ends without marriage will the man or the woman be most hurt? Why?

Is it possible to love more than one person at a time? Why?

"In life there is one thing that everyone wants and this is love." Is this true?

Should love be hidden?

References and Notes

1. Margery Perham, *The Government of Ethiopia* (New York: Oxford University Press, 1948).
2. "Creating a popular, economic, political and military base" (Unpublished EPLF document, 1982).
3. Gebre-Medhin, Jordan, *Peasants and Nationalism in Eritrea* (New Jersey: Red Sea Press Inc., 1989).
4. Silkin, Trish, in Report for CAFOD on the Mogoraib-Forto Community Development Project 1990 (unpublished).
5. Two important aspects of the struggle in Eritrea have not been dealt with in this book. The first is the subject of famine, which has been extensively documented for the Horn of Africa by non-governmental organizations and also by the Eritrean Relief Association, a body set up by the EPLF. The second is the situation of people who have become refugees and have had to leave Eritrea.
6. Rava, M, "Ovest Etiopico: nei paesi del platino e dell' oro", *Nuova Antologica* (1938). cited in Pankhurst, Richard, "Italian and 'native' labour during the Italian fascist occupation of Ethiopia 1935-41" *Ghana Social Science Journal*, vol. 2, no. 2, pp. 42- 73 (1972).
7. Compared with British or French colonies of a similar type, the line dividing the jobs done by European and African workers was drawn much lower in Eritrea. This was because Italian capitalism was less developed and unemployment was very high in Italy. The late nineteenth century European drive for colonies in Africa arose out of the need of mature capitalist countries to export capital. Italy, on the other hand, was less mature and

had no capital to export. It substituted capitalist drive with what Gramsci calls "the strong popular passions blindly intent on possessing land".
8. Giuglia, G., "Lineamenti economici del nuova Impero (Genova 1938), quoted in Pankhurst, Richard, "Italian and "native" labour during the Italian fascists occupation of Ethiopia 1935-41", *Ghana Social Science Journal*, vol. 2, no. 2, pp. 42-73 (1972).
9. This was the approach of De Bono, the Italian High Commissioner of Eritrea, cited in Pankhurst, Richard, "Italian and 'native' labour during the Italian fascist occupation of Ethiopia 1935- 41", *Ghana Social Science Journal*, vol. 2, no. 2, pp. 42-73 (date).
10. Gebre-Medhin, Jordan, *Peasants and Nationalism in Eritrea* (New Jersey: Red Sea Press Inc. 1989).
11. Hiwet added: "Working as a domestic with a British family was also hard but at least they treated one as a worker with fixed hours, not as a servant or slave as the Italians did."
12. Tresvaskis, G.K.N., *Eritrea: A Colony in Transition* Oxford University Press, (London: 1960)
13. Document of the second Congress of the EPLF (the Unity Congress) in March 1987.
14. Markakis, John and Nega Ayele, *Class and Revolution in Ethiopia* (Nottingham: Spokesman, 1978).
15. Why should women be more involved in a national struggle than in a class struggle? Worku did not expand on this, but the reality is borne out by many anti-colonial struggles. Perhaps it is because too often women's productive labour – in the fields, for example – is disregarded, and their labour in production and rearing of children and servicing of male workers is relegated to the realm of "natural activities". Women are not therefore seen as members of the working class, whereas no one can deny their national identity – in fact their "natural activities" make them central to the propagation of the nation.
16. From February 1974 onwards the radical students and intelligentsia started addressing leaflets to all sections of the population including the military. They hoped for a rebellion in the armed forces, but at the same time were afraid of military

intervention on behalf of the regime. When the Dergue seized military control of the state it had to pretend initially to be part of the radical movement simply because of its massive popularity. This gave it a chance to pre-empt the revolution and establish itself in power.

17. In areas where political education has been insufficient, a people's committee is sometimes set up. It consists of fifteen to twenty members from a variety of class backgrounds, and undertakes simple administrative tasks. In areas which are only partially liberated or have only recently come under EPLF control there are smaller committees of four or five people, called resistance committees.

18. "Creating a popular, economic, political and military base", unpublished EPLF document, 1982.

19. Gramsci, Antonio, *Selections from the Prison Notebooks* (London: Lawrence and Wishart, 1971).

20. Zemheret Yohannes who joined the ELF in 1975, was in the leadership of the splinter group called the ELF-CL and is now in the Central Committee of the EPLF, told Philip Gottlieb in an interview:

> The experience of the ELF can be divided into two basic stages: first 1961 to 1970 and second 1970 to 1981. In the first stage the ELF was not an organisation in the strict sense . . . it did not have a democratically elected leadership, it did not have a clearly drawn political line or organisational constitution. . . . After the split in 1970 and the establishment of the EPLF, the ruling circle of the ELF were compelled by the new development to make political concessions. . . . The ruling circle knew that they could not continue in the old way, and in 1971, at the first Congress, the ELF adopted its first programme. Theoretically it was a National Democratic Programme, and at least formally, a leadership was elected and a general political line and strategy was at least theoretically drawn

up. But the ruling circle, the traditionalist leadership . . . did not change. This was the basic weakness – the basic negative factor which ten years later was to drive the ELF into oblivion. (Personal communication, Philip Gottleib).
21. Fanon, Frantz, *The Wretched of the Earth* (Harmondsworth, Middlesex: Penguin, 1967).
22. This was part of the populist measures undertaken by the Dergue in its early years.
23. Unpublished interview of Saba Asier by Jenneke Arens 1986.
24. *Dispatches*, Channel 4, June 1990.
25. The dispute over whether the region of Ogaden belonged to Somalia or Ethiopia was finally resolved in a peace treaty in 1985. After that Ethiopia pulled out those divisions of the army stationed in Ogaden and used them against the EPLF.
26. *Selected Works of Zhou Enlai*, vol. 1, *Launch a Nationwide Counter Offensive to Overthrow Chiang Kai-Shek* (location: publisher, date), p. 304.
27. "Experiences of the EPLF in Pursuing the policy of self reliance in the economic field", unpublished EPLF document, 1982.
28. Firebrace, James and Stuart Holland, *Never Kneel Down* (Nottingham: Spokesman, 1984).
29. *Adulis*, vol. V, no. 5 (date) (published by the Foreign Relations Bureau of the Eritrean People's Liberation Front – European and North American Desks).
30. The Makelai Aliet are immigrants from Ethiopia to the highlands. They are Tigrinya-speaking Coptic Christians but are regarded as outsiders because they do not belong to the clans which originally lived in these villages. As such they have very few rights.
31. Enda is the basic kinship unit in the highland villages.
32. The term "serf" is used rather loosely by writers on Eritrea: it does not always correspond to its usual meaning with respect to relations of production.
33. Plowden, W., *Travels in Abyssinia* (London:, 1868).
34. Slavery is mentioned occasionally in rural areas but as a mode of production it was overtaken by emerging feudalism. It probably originated when members of one group were captured by another and enslaved. As such it has nothing to do with

the slave trade and has not caused any permanent divisions in Eritrean society.

35. The Maria Therese thaler was the currency used in Eritrea as well as Ethiopia, though in rural areas wage labour was extremely rare. One Maria Therese thaler was a large sum of money, almost half the monthly salary of the Ethiopian emperor's bodyguards.

36. "Creating a popular, economic, political and military base" (unpublished EPLF document, 1982).

37. EPLF National Democratic Programme 1977.

38. Kelkar, Govind, *Women and Rural Economic Reform in China*, Occasional Papers on History and Society, Nehru Memorial Museum and Library, New Delhi, 1989.

39. Feudal ideologies can become incorporated into new social formations.

40. Hamiens are women minstrels who sing and then demand payment; they signify the beginning of feudalism in Eritrea.

41. Silkin, Trish, M. Phil. thesis, University of London, 1990.

42. For example, according to Maharite and Gaddam, among Catholic Billens:

> Most girls are virgins but if a girl is not a virgin, her husband cannot send her away – religion forbids this. He tells his friends and they stand on the roof and pour water on her house so that everybody comes to know about it. Then they cut a hole in the curtain of her room. Her husband can beat her but in time they live together and forget.

43. Most Kunamas are animists but there is a Muslim minority.

44. Trish Silkin quotes the following folk story in her thesis:[41]

> In the Red Sea area there was once a religious leader called Monisa. She was head of the Mosque. Allah wanted to test her fidelity and tempted her through a naked devil who waited for her on the way to the mosque. On the first day she ignored his enticements. The same happened the next day. But on the third day she slept with him and arrived late at the Mosque. The Lord cursed her from then onwards. Women were consequently banned from entering the Mosque, confined to their homes and compelled to wear veils. They were to be subordinate to their husbands.

45. In the southern highlands (this includes Akele Guzai and parts of Hamasen) where the EPLF was very popular from the mid-1970s, the laws were reformed as early as 1978. However, the Ethiopians succeeded in penetrating the area again in the early 1980s and this meant that people had to be extremely cautious about applying the new law in case they were identified as EPLF supporters.

46. "Meeting the needs of the present and building for the future – primary health care in Rural Eritrea, Eritrean Public Health Programme, London.

47. "Drugs Policy and Pharmaceutical Services in Eritrea," Yohannes Fassil, in *Proceedings of the First International Conference on Health in Eritrea*, Milan, 1–2 November 1986, published by the Eritrean Public Health Programme, discusses among other topics the advantages of the local formulation of essential drugs:

> It saves time; it is cheaper to buy raw materials in bulk and formulate them locally; it has an added advantage in producing the required dosage and amount at the right time i.e. in times of epidemic and high incidences of certain diseases such as malaria and meningitis; it is a big step forwards for the development of local pharmaceutical technology in minimizing dependence and enhancing self sufficiency.

48. The EPHP plastic microscope (original design by Dr John McArthur) has been introduced in several countries including the Philippines, Bangladesh, India, Mozambique, Brazil, Mexico and Egypt.

49. The Barka region has lagged behind others in this respect. In Report for CAFOD on "the Nara of Mogoraib and the Beni Amer of Forto (Lower Barka): Implications for the Mogoraib-Forto Community Development Project' (1990, unpublished), Trish Silkin writes:

> While in other parts of the country women do now have their own union and they have also been elected as members of the People's Committees, in Mogoraib and Forto women have not yet formed a union and as a result they are able to neither vote nor stand in

election. This low level of organisation partly reflects the EPLF's relatively recent presence in the area, but also the influence of the ELF. ELF propaganda against the EPLF is particularly strong in its old stronghold of Barka, and has tended to focus on the EPLF's efforts to mobilise women.

Index

Abdullah, Ali Haji 87
Abraham, Asmeret ("Gwandi") 74-5, 100-2, 143-4, 154
Abrahed, health worker 146-8
Algeria 63
Amahatzion, guerrilla 76
Andom, Yemane and Memhir 76
Ari, Fatna 87-9, 109
Asier, Saba 73, 76-7

Bakheet, Sembatu 68-9, 123, 136-8
bar-women 11, 80-6
bride prices 123-6
British exploitation of Eritrea 7, 17-21, 117

"Challenge Road" 104
China 121, 134
Chu chu, cadre 97-9
churches and reform 118 137-8
circumcision, female 7, 115, 127-8, 137-8
colonialism
  British 17-21
  Italian 4-5, 10-18

Dattabulla, fighter 69-70
Debssai, Mahari 94
Dergue (Ethiopian junta) 8, 41, 45-6, 70, 117, 200n
  genocide in Eritrea 70-2, 87-8, 102, 143-4
  Red Star Campaign (sixth offensive) 102, 105
  refusal of negotiations 106
  Stealth Offensive (seventh) 105-6
  torture of women 76-80
dowries/bride prices 27, 58, 65, 123-6, 130

Dulles, John Foster 21-2

education 178
Eritrea
  annexation by Ethiopia (1962) 8, 26
  civil war (1972-4) 47, 48
  federation with Ethiopia (1950) 7, 22-3
  history 2-4
  see also ELF; EPLF; women
Eritrean Liberation Front (ELF) (1961) 25-6, 30-1, 35-6, 38-40, 47-8, 55, 90-1, 200-1n, 203-4n
  internal dissent/killings 33, 41, 47, 94
  and women's participation 40, 57-60
Eritrean Liberation Movement (ELM) *see* Group of Seven
Eritrean People's Liberation Front (EPLF) (1970) 2, 31-3, 40, 47, 90-1
  "Behind the Enemy Lines" strategy 72-86
  Department of Mass Administration 47-9, 72
  as fighting force 93-110
  future aims 152-4
  and health care 140-9
  and land reform 111-21, 180-2
  and marriage reform 122-38, 185-93, 194-7
  National Democratic Programme (January 1977) 99, 120, 155-65
  National Democratic Programme (March 1987) 166-77
  organizational structure 183
  people's assemblies 49-54, 119, 145

people's militias 54–6, 118–19
and political education 95–8, 118, 134, 200n
and self-reliance 103–4, 142–3, 145, 203n
on violence 90–1
women's participation 49–52, 55–61, 96–9, 184–5
Ethiopia
annexes Eritrea (1962) 8, 26, 66
federation with Eritrea (1950) 7–8, 22–3
imposes Amharic language 23–4
power structure in 8
see also Dergue
Ethiopian People's Revolutionary Party (EPRP) (1973) 45–7

family structure 5–7, 8
famine 45
Fanon, Frantz 62–4, 69, 71
Fassaha, Gedey ("Gandhi") 30

Gebrai, Elsa 127
Georgis, Hiwet Ogba 15–16, 93–5, 150–1, 199n
Georgis, Petros 41–5, 47, 64, 75–6
Germatsion, Teberh 53–5
Ghdy, cadre 57–61
Gidai, Woldai 94
Girmai, Abrahedsien 120, 148–9, 153–4
Gramsci, Antonio 56
Group of Seven (1958) 25, 29–31, 35, 41, 63

Habte, Haddas 94–5
Habte, "Adei" Ogba 33–4, 36–9
Habtomeu, "Abba" 89–90
Hagos, Masfin 94
Haile, ex-prisoner of war 91–2
Hailemariam, Davit 27–8, 130
Hailu, Lemlem 13–14, 52–3, 71
Hajaji, Akiar 124
health problems and health care 139–49

Ibrahim, Zainab 126–7, 130
India, marriage principles 122–5, 127, 129
Indrias, Sara 65, 124
infibulation 7, 115, 127–8, 137–8, 146

Italy/Italian
colonialism 4–5, 10–18, 112–13, 116, 198–9n
conquers Eritrea and Ethiopia 3–4, 17

Kahsai, Ande Michael 24, 25, 47–9, 73–4, 95, 133–4, 152
Kassa, Mabrat 9–32
Kiflu, Kidane 94–5

land reform 111–21, 180–2
Linesh, health worker 144

Maaza, cadre 1, 90
Makelai, Aliet 112, 201n
Mandar, Saida 108–9
Mao Zedong 91
Marasani, Paulino 16
marriage reform 111, 122–38, 185–93, 194–7
Mebrahtu, Martha 47
Mengistu Haile Mariam, Colonel 67, 70–1, 87, 105, 109–10, 150
Menkarios, Askalu 34, 88–9, 154
Meza, fighter 69–70
Michael, Dr Nerayo Tekle 128, 140–2
Millet, Kate 80
Mohamed, Hamida Ahmad 131
Mozambique 120
Muslim League (1946) 21, 35–6

National Union of Eritrean Women (NUEW) 49–50, 88–9, 104, 154, 184
nationalism 69
Nebiat, bar-woman 82–5
Nech Lebash militia 55–7, 74

Okobalidet, Gaddam 67
Omer, Fatma 6, 39–40, 52, 113, 115–16, 146
Ona massacre (1970) 68
orphans 89–90

Party of Love of Country (PLC) 19–21
patriarchialism 5–7, 123, 126–7, 129–30, 199n
Petros, Dr 71–2
prostitution 11, 13–14, 27, 42

Index   207

Red Peasant Marches 92
Russom, Engineer 76

Sabe, Othman 29
Selassie, Haile 7-8, 26-7, 41-2, 44, 114
Shembera, Amna Mohamed 109-10
Society for the Unification of Eritrea and Ethiopia (SUEE) (1944) 19
Soviet Union support for Dergue 46, 88, 99-100, 105
student participation in revolution 41-5, 58, 178, 199-200n
Sudan Defence Force (SDF) Incident (1946) 20

Tekhle, Maharite 67, 128-9, 153
Teklai, Lieutenant 75
Terafic, Ibrahim 29-30
Tigrayan People's Liberation Front (TPLF) 110, 200n

Unionist Party (1946) 21, 35-6
United Nations 7, 21-2
United States 7, 21-2, 26-7
    support for Ethiopia 41-2, 46, 88

Vero, Dr 22

Waliling, Ethiopian student 45, 47
Wind, Tsegat 77-80
Wolde-Mariam, Ato Wolde-Ab 19-21, 24-5

Woldu, Askalou 50-2
women
    bar-women 11, 80-6
    and "Behind the Enemy Lines" strategy 72-86
    circumcision/infibulation 7, 115, 127-8, 137-8, 146
    impact of colonialism on 5
    and land reform 111-21, 180-2
    and marriage reform 111, 122-38, 185-97
    maternal mortality 147
    oppression/sexual exploitation of 9, 11, 13-17, 27-8, 36-9, 58-60, 64-5, 80-3, 115-16, 124-5, 130, 153, 202n
    and patriarchialism 5-7, 123, 126-7, 129-30, 199n
    and people's assemblies 50-5
    and people's militias 54-7
    torture by the Dergue 76-80
    see also EPLF; NUEW; Women's Association
Women's Association 51-2
Workers' Syndicate (1958) 25

Yihedego, Maasho and Tukhu 94-5
Yohannes, Zemheret 200-1n

Zaid, fighter 69-70
Zerai, Worku 24-5, 34, 44, 46-7, 96-7, 199n